CULTURE
IN THE CITY

SUNDERLAND'S CULTURAL
TRANSFORMATION

CULTURE IN THE CITY

SUNDERLAND'S CULTURAL TRANSFORMATION

Edited by
Paul Callaghan

Contributors

David Allan
Rebecca Ball
Paul Callaghan
Richard Callaghan
Kam Chera
Helen Connify
Peter Darrant
Kristian Foreman
Helen Green
Keith Gregson
Daniel Krzyszczak
Rob Lawson

Carol McKay
Hannah Matterson
Keith Merrin
Ross Millard
John Mowbray
Padma Rao
Amanda Ritson
Alistair Robinson
Iain Rowan
Julia Stephenson
Graeme Thompson
Paul Watson

MACSunderland
Music, Arts and Culture Trust

First published in 2017 by the Sunderland Music, Arts and Culture Trust
in association with My World Publishing
Chase House
4 Mandarin Road
Rainton Bridge
Houghton le Spring,
Sunderland DH4 5RA
United Kingdom

CULTURE IN THE CITY

ISBN: 978 1 909486 26 3

Printed and bound in North East England by Martins the Printers Ltd.

Contents

Introduction

This book is a celebration of the cultural transformation that the City of Sunderland is currently experiencing. If this book had been written a decade or two ago it would have been a much slimmer volume for while much of the city's cultural history and heritage that we celebrate in these pages can be traced back over the centuries, it is in this last decade that the city has begun to regain both its cultural confidence and capacity.

What has been most remarkable over this period is how much Sunderland's cultural offering has diversified its audiences, its contributors and its genres. The city now hosts an International Film festival, the UK's Graphic Novel Expo, music festivals, celebrations of Asian and Eastern European art, national and international exhibitions in glass and fine art, West End shows and so much more, as well as music, drama and arts and crafts groups thriving in social clubs and community centres, often as a consequence of the city's Cultural Spring.

As this book shows, Sunderland is a place with so many creative people: painters, poets, musicians and glassmakers, people who want to create art and culture and a population who increasingly want to enjoy it. Individual artists, writers and performers are gaining national and international exposure and in so doing they are encouraging the growing ambition and self-belief of the generations that follow.

The contributors to this book share a common belief that culture, in all its diverse forms, makes our city a better place. It enriches the lives of the people who live here or who visit our city, it creates greater opportunities for our children and young people and enhances Sunderland's image and reputation. By creating an environment where many different cultural forms can flourish, our city becomes more diverse, vibrant, interesting, stimulating and a place where talent wants to live.

Many people have been involved in this production and I'd particularly like to thank Tim Murphy from courage creative who, with the help of Daniel Cain, designed this beautiful book, and David Allan whose has contributed many of the wonderful photographs included here. A full list of the individual contributors of both the words and the images are listed at the end of the book.

Finally, thank you to Dorothy for her limitless patience, love and support.

Paul Callaghan

Book Cover Images

The front cover top image is of Martin Longstaff, a multi-instrumentalist and songwriter from Sunderland who performs as the Lake Poets. His moving performance at the Summer Streets Festival was wonderfully photographed by Dan Prince.

The front cover bottom image is of the Royal Philharmonic Orchestra rehearsing at the Sunderland Empire before a Sound Around relaxed family concert produced by Orchestras Live aimed at engaging young people with orchestral music. The scene was captured beautifully by photographer, David Allan.

Commissioned by the North East Photography Network (NEPN), the image on the back cover is Julian Germain's Newborns. As part of Sunderland's cultural transformation, Julian Germain photographed babies born on Wearside in the summer of 2015. As representatives of Sunderland's newest citizens, the photographs not only ask us to consider the mystery of being human but also the mystery of the future, what will it hold for them? The babies' images are framed in the doors of the city's old Fire Station, which at that time stood empty and derelict. It has now been renovated and restored as the centrepiece of the city's Music, Arts and Culture Quarter.

Why Culture? Why Sunderland?

WORDS BY *Kristian Foreman*
& Paul Callaghan
Sunderland Music, Arts & Culture Trust

Why Culture? Why Sunderland?

"culture plays a central role in most twenty-first century cities"

Culture plays a central role in most twenty-first century cities and this book will look specifically at the part it plays today in the city of Sunderland and, more importantly, at the role it can play in the future. First, however, let us consider the general question of why art and culture is important and what is its role in contemporary society?

In Paris in 1833, artist, poet, and novelist Theophile Gautier argued that art is an end in itself and used an expression that has since been widely quoted. His phrase "L'art pour l'art" or in English "art for art's sake" emphatically states that its purpose is artistic and not for other reasons. Yet this book will challenge this. In today's complex world, "art for art's sake" is only one element of what culture can deliver. In fact, the importance of art and culture is that it can be a means to achieve other ends that touch not just the artistic soul of the individual but have a much wider impact on society as a whole. Culture can be used as a sophisticated tool to strengthen social cohesion, increase personal confidence and improve life skills. It feeds into the economy, health and learning. It can help us to communicate our inner world, cope with things like loneliness and fill us with hope. It can strengthen our ability to act as empathetic and democratic citizens at the same time as creating innovative training and new employment routes. Culture has always mattered and today it matters more than ever for our cities. It helps give a place its values and identity. It inspires, empowers and elevates those who live, work, and enjoy the city and it should be placed at the centre of economic and social regeneration.

Culture is a notoriously difficult term to define so what exactly do we mean when we refer to it? It can of course have different meanings in different contexts. We may describe a person as 'cultured', meaning they have good taste or a good education, while using 'culture' in reference to a community or group we often mean a set of shared values, of the way we

Why Culture? Why Sunderland?

do things and understand things and this may be seen as a 'cultural identity' that binds a community together and is often formed by the peculiar historical development of that community. Yet when we use the word 'culture' as an activity, we often mean in it in terms of art, literature, music, dance, film and so on. In this book, the main emphasis is on this third meaning, looking at the impact cultural activity has on the development of cities in general and Sunderland in particular. We will be looking at the production, consumption, and economic value of culture, as well as its use as a tool for urban regeneration and place-shaping. We will also be looking at culture as a process, something that inspires creativity and innovation, changing individuals as well as places.

Take a moment to imagine a world without music, cinema, dance, literature and poetry. A world without the albums of The Beatles or the compositions of Beethoven, the movies of Hitchcock or the paintings of Monet; without Shakespeare, Dickens or Tennessee Williams. That world would be a very dull place devoid of imagination and inspiration. Our shared human creativity and the ability to create art and culture is one of the things that distinguishes us as human beings and binds us all together. It is what makes living worthwhile. So why would people choose to live, work and study in cities that don't support arts and culture?

Theatres, galleries, cinemas, libraries, or concert halls are all integral parts of a thriving city as they create a vibrancy in communities, entertainment for its residents, and a source of happiness and inspiration. Every city needs to have a cultural soul. It needs to have opportunities where people can develop their cultural talents. A place where people can go to see or create great art. A place that helps other people realise that their own creativity is important and inspires them. One of the biggest drivers of a successful city is confidence and culture can provide this.

But creating a cultural city is not just about infrastructure, it is also about the activity that goes on there such as concerts, exhibitions, design competitions or children's craft workshops that promote expression, celebration and achievement and embody the values and identity of a place, cultural activities that express local distinctiveness and that encourage civic pride. What is more, citizens are empowered through the creation of civic pride and social cohesion, and they feel more connected and content towards the city. It can also bring prosperity by attracting visitors, investors and people who wish to study or live in the city. It can drive high growth creative businesses and stimulate both a day-time and night-time economy that have benefits that are far wider than those enjoyed by the artists or the venues. Culture tends to spread

Why Culture? Why Sunderland?

prosperity much wider through society as it creates jobs and opportunities and adds to people's confidence and pride in where they live.

Investment in culture has historically been seen as an investment in promoting public good rather than benefiting the economy and often something that can only be invested in during prosperous times and not justifiable when the economy is struggling. However, it is important to recognise arts, culture and creativity as a burgeoning economic sector that consistently generates jobs, creates tourism and generally makes more money for our economy than it costs to fund.

So from an economic standpoint, we need a society that puts arts and culture at the heart of its cities. John Kampfner, Chief Executive of the Creative Industries Federation, says spending money on the arts is crucial for the good of society, he comments "There is nothing 'nice to have' about the arts and the creative industries, there is nothing tangential, nothing 'soft'. They are central to our economy, our public life and our nation's health".

Cultural and creative industries are typically labour-intensive; they are businesses that employ people in the community and purchase local goods and services. They are rooted locally; providing jobs that cannot be done anywhere but in their own cities. They are good business citizens that should be encouraged and supported wherever possible.

The economic benefits do not end with increased employment. Cultural activity exponentially increases footfall and spending within cities. Cultural audiences spend a lot of money in their city. Think about the last time you went to a cultural event - whether it was a concert, the cinema, or an open mic gig at your local pub. As well as buying your ticket you may have spent money on parking, transport, eating dinner at a local restaurant beforehand or having a drink afterwards. There is lots of economic activity that is related to that cultural event. As well as the cultural sector making money, local businesses such as restaurants, hotels, retailers profit too. Such businesses are also great for tourism as they often spend a lot of resources focusing on marketing and promoting the cities in which they exist. Cultural offerings make cities very attractive for tourists, both non-locally and internationally and cities that can draw tourists experience a considerable additional boost to economic activity.

Cities that want to compete in the global market should appreciate art and culture not only for its aesthetic and entertainment value, but in particular because it invigorates creativity and innovation that could potentially lead to commercialised products and ideas. Rather than focusing on short term fixes, cities should create an environment that fosters creativity and innovation. As Ian Livingstone, co-founder of Games Workshop and former Chairman of Eidos said "We are all only as good as our last creative idea. If we want to be a country of innovators we need to be constantly creative.

Why Culture? Why Sunderland?

To become creative, innovative and imaginative, we need to expose ourselves to new ideas. A vibrant arts and culture community is the easiest way to make this happen […] We have to stop thinking about arts and culture as simply nice to have. They are just as important as well-maintained roads and bridges. By giving us the chance to stimulate our minds with new ideas and experiences, they give us the opportunity to become more creative. Arts and culture are infrastructure for the mind." Furthermore, american economist, Richard Florida, argues that creativity is our greatest resource in today's post-industrial climate. The ability to harness and nurture our creativity is an essential component to maintaining wealth and prosperity in cities.

Art and culture isn't just a thing that provides us with entertainment and profit - in the words of Oscar Wilde, we don't want to live in a society that "knows the price of everything and the value of nothing". Arts and culture are the means by which we express ourselves, connect to other people, share experiences and discover new things about ourselves, each other and the wider world around us. Culture holds a power that allows us to be more rounded, balanced, sane and empathetic citizens in all parts of our life. This type of personal impact, however, is very difficult to prove and quantify. The fact of the matter is that it is very difficult to answer the question "How does art impact people and society?" Due to its subtle and latent ways, it is extremely difficult to quantify and qualify how culture affects those that engage with it on a personal level. This intangible value is both its beauty as well as its disadvantage. This intangibility often creates difficulty when trying to convince politicians of the importance of arts funding, since the importance,

Why Culture? Why Sunderland?

"Prosperity leads to ambition and optimism. This encourages and drives educational attainment. This in turn enriches and diversifies the city's culture"

significance and merit of the arts cannot be judged by popular consensus and numbers alone. Culture should be something that matters to everyone. It is for the masses, not the few. It is a right, not a privilege. It creates opportunity and hope for everyone who wants it, and sometimes a pleasant surprise to those who didn't know how much they would enjoy it. It is a belief system. As Article 27 of the Universal Declaration of Human rights states: "Everyone has the right freely to participate in the cultural life of the community, to enjoy the arts and to share in scientific advancement and its benefits."

Cities are becoming more and more diverse in this globalised world. Each place has a mix of different races, genders, classes, ages and backgrounds all living under one roof.

Cities, towns and communities are built on three separate but interrelated pillars: a successful economy, a good education system for all and a rich and vibrant culture. These three elements create a virtuous circle. Prosperity leads to ambition and optimism. This encourages and drives educational attainment. This in turn enriches and diversifies the city's culture. The city's vibrant culture stimulates prosperity and so on. Of course, the reverse is true. A failing economy lowers expectations and aspirations leading to falling educational attainment, further depressing the economy. People, often the most able and the most talented, leave and so the demand for and supply of culture falls. The place enters a vicious circle of decline from which it is difficult to extract itself.

So why should we encourage and invest in arts and culture in poorer areas of the country like Sunderland, rather than focusing attention and funding on those places that are already succeeding, that already have the cultural

infrastructure and high cultural participation rates? This is not an equity argument - although it easily could be. No, this is a social and economic argument. The right to access or participate in great art and culture should not be a function of where you are born or where you live. It should be there for all, irrespective of socio-economic standing or postcode. The most creative people often come from the most unexpected places and by widening participation and investing in the arts and creative industries we can take culture and creativity into the heart of communities and fundamentally change places forever. It will come as no surprise that the areas with the lowest participation rates in arts, culture and creativity are also the poorest communities, places with significant physical and mental health issues, low educational achievement levels and challenges of social cohesion.

Sunderland is a city that is undergoing significant change and this transformation is having a marked effect on the psyche of the city, as well as on the attitude of its citizens. With a population of 275,000, Sunderland is the 18th largest city in the country and is a place of growing aspiration, growing expectation and growing demand for cultural opportunities. The publication of the City's Cultural Strategy in 2014 was a clear statement of this growing ambition, yet Sunderland has also been a place that has in the past been poorly served in terms of both cultural infrastructure and cultural provision.

It is a place of working class poets and writers whose literature has been drawn and shaped by the lives they live. People who have no history of family artistic participation but who become dancers and musicians because someone opened a door for them, a door to another world, a world

that they then realised they wanted to inhabit. So, who opened that door? It might have been a teacher, a friend or an organisation but without that door being opened their life would have been poorer, perhaps not financially, but certainly culturally and spiritually.

For many people in Sunderland there had been a poor 'cultural offer' for generations. No one has 'opened' that cultural door for them. Yet in a city like Sunderland a relatively modest investment can produce phenomenal results. The Cultural Spring, Arts Council England's Creative People and Places programme in Sunderland, has taken art, artists, creativity and creators into the communities of those that are culturally least active. The results are extraordinary. People who were waiting to have culture offered to them grab it with both hands. But more significant is the reaction of those who thought art and culture 'wasn't for the likes of us'. They find they can play a musical instrument, paint a picture, invent and create. They find modern dance is exhilarating, classical music is enchanting or impressionist art can touch their soul. The door has been opened and for some, even for many, it will change their lives forever.

Yet more than a thousand years ago, it was culture that was of such significance to Sunderland. It was from the monastery at Monkwearmouth-Jarrow in about AD 731 that the Venerable Bede wrote the Ecclesiastical History of the English People, in Latin 'Historia ecclesiastica gentis Anglorum'. A history of the Christian Churches in England, and of England generally, it is considered to be one of the most important original references on Anglo-Saxon history and has played a key role in the development of an English national identity. This work gave purpose, pride and identity to a growing local community as well as making an unprecedented impact on a global scale.

Today, thirteen centuries after Bede, Sunderland's cultural renaissance will reinstate culture at the core of Sunderland's economy and community, acting as the catalyst for significant and enduring social and economic change within the city and from the city to the region and the world. Just as Bede's innovative perspective transformed the time and the world in which he lived, so this vision seeks to harness the transformative potential of culture by embedding it at the heart of the regeneration and rebirth of a city that has suffered more than three decades of deindustrialisation and economic decline. The population of Sunderland is becoming more educated, more aspirational and more likely to take advantage of cultural opportunities. For example, in the decade between 2004 and 2014, the percentage of Sunderland's working age population with qualifications at NVQ Level 4 and higher rose from 15% to 24% and during the same period Sunderland's student population rose significantly. Yet despite the rise in educational standards

Why Culture? Why Sunderland?

> **"This vision seeks to harness the transformative potential of culture by embedding it at the heart of the regeneration and rebirth of a city."**

Sunderland still faces major economic challenges. The 2011 Census showed Sunderland with significantly higher levels of unemployment, higher levels of long-term disability, and a greater number of people in lower socio-economic groups than the national average. Despite this, the census also showed 42.7% of the city's population in intermediate occupations or higher.

Sunderland's population has until quite recently been offered relatively few cultural opportunities for a city of its size and population, and yet when such opportunities do arise, as demonstrated by the Cultural Spring, Sunderland Stages and the investment in the National Glass Centre, they prove successful. This is because they are tapping into a source of unmet demand, a base of consumers who are waiting for a programme of consistent and reliable cultural events with which they can engage. In addition to the large base of potential cultural consumers already existing within the city, Sunderland can also boast a number of successful cultural

Kristian Foreman & Paul Callaghan

"Sunderland represents one of the greatest opportunities for culturally driven change in Britain today"

producers, artists who export their work from the city. Musicians like the Futureheads, Field Music and the Lake Poets have, in recent years, gained recognition on a national and international stage whilst carrying with them a strong sense of their role as representatives and cultural ambassadors for Sunderland and the North East as a whole. This talent needs to be harnessed for the benefit of both the city and the artists themselves.

Sunderland represents one of the greatest opportunities for culturally driven change in Britain today. The cultural vision for the future of Sunderland is one which seeks to take advantage of this opportunity, to enhance the life of the city, to empower its citizens, to use the knowledge and talent and creativity and skill of Sunderland's people to continue the work already being done within the city, and to ensure Sunderland retains a vibrant cultural future. The future for Sunderland will see performance, rehearsal and development spaces as well as a culture and arts programme that attracts audiences, encourages and develops indigenous talent and becomes a magnet for artists and arts organisations both to perform and show but also to locate in a city with such a vibrant and thriving cultural centre. Sunderland will become a place where 'talent wants to be'. Sunderland can boast a number of significant and successful cultural events and projects including the Cultural Spring, Summer Streets Festival, Sunderland Stages, and Wonderlands. These events have been a success because they have been embraced by the people of Sunderland, as well as making Sunderland a cultural destination for visitors from around the region. The success of these projects demonstrates that when presented with opportunities for cultural participation, the people of Sunderland engage enthusiastically and creatively with artistic and cultural projects. This fact is the core motivation for the development of a cultural vision for the future of Sunderland.

One other feature that sets Sunderland apart is that important stakeholders, the University, City Council, key cultural organisations like the MAC Trust and business, cultural and community organisations are all working together, following the same strategy and pursuing the same cultural goals. This cooperation and cohesion of purpose allows Sunderland to focus resources, time and expertise on ensuring that those goals are met. Through cultural development we can change Sunderland and its people in a number of ways, for example:

- Help the city and particularly its young people to grow more confident, raise aspiration and attainment levels and create many more opportunities to develop.

- Build a more inclusive city and tackle issues of discrimination, loneliness and social isolation.

- Create a healthier city and increase the wellbeing of all of Sunderland's residents.

- Create a better city in which to live and work, embedding sustainable social change as central to Sunderland's future.

The cultural multiplier, the return from focusing attention, encouragement and investment is so much greater in Sunderland because here culture is not just a 'nice to have', it is a fundamental game-changer. For Sunderland, arts and culture is an incredible force of regeneration, both culturally and economically. It has a positive relationship with health, crime, society, education, confidence and well-being. It isn't an 'either/or' situation, it is an 'as well as' situation. Cities like Sunderland operate in an intensely competitive market. All want to attract business, people, investment, resources, and talent and having a prominent arts and culture scene feeds into all of these areas and so needs investment and development. Vibrant cities offer an array of cultural qualities that creates desirable places to live, work, invest, produce and enjoy and the more access to culture that Sunderland has, the better it will be.

Kristian Foreman & Paul Callaghan

Why Culture? Why Sunderland?

Kristian Foreman & Paul Callaghan

Sunderland's Performance Venues

Sunderland Empire Theatre

The Empire Palace, as it was then known, was opened in 1907. Established by South Shields born theatre owner and impresario Richard Thornton, the Empire was designed by leading Sunderland architects William and Thomas Milburn and opened by leading music hall star Vesta Tilley. Topped by a ninety-foot tower with a statue of Terpsichore, the Greek muse of dance and choral song, the following century has seen the Empire's stage graced by some of the biggest names in entertainment.

Tommy Steele made his stage debut at the Empire in November 1957, whilst the Beatles played the Empire on their first UK tour. Helen Mirren's first stage appearance came at the Empire, whilst it was also the site of Sid James's last, the heart attack he suffered on stage during a performance of The Mating Season causing his death in 1976.

James is just one of three ghosts said to haunt the Empire, the other two being Vesta Tilley and Molly Moselle. Moselle, assistant stage manager on a 1949 production of Ivor Novello's The Dancing Years, went to buy a birthday card on the afternoon of January 14 that year and was never seen again.

The Empire, now with over 1800 seats and a total capacity of 2,200, remains the city's most significant performance venue, as well as the only theatre in the region capable of staging transfers of large scale shows from London's West End.

Stalls and
Vesta Tilley Bars

No Smoking

Richard Callaghan

The Royalty Theatre

One of the North East's oldest amateur theatre groups, the Royalty Theatre in Sunderland was founded in 1925 as the Sunderland Drama Club. The inaugural meeting took place at Meng's Restaurant on Fawcett Street, with performances taking place at the Victoria Hall. In 1930, funds were raised to open the "Little Theatre" on Tavistock Place, at a cost of £1,178.3s.0d. It opened in 1931 and was used to stage private performances, with the Victoria Hall continuing to host the Drama Club's main shows.

The Victoria Hall and the "Little Theatre" were destroyed by German bombing in 1941. This forced the Drama Club's performances to move to, amongst other places, the Royalty Hall. From 1946, the Royalty Hall became the Drama Club's home after a lease was negotiated which enabled the use of the hall and three other rooms.

The late 1960s saw the club become owners of The Royalty, taking control of the hall and making it the club's permanent home. In 1994 the club's name was changed to Royalty Theatre Sunderland.

Arts Centre Washington

Washington was designated a "New Town" in 1964, part of the movement to foster economic growth and create better living conditions for the population overspilling from the North East's larger and more established cities and towns. Fifteen numbered districts were designated, with new infrastructure constructed throughout the existing villages in the hope of generating new jobs. The masterplan for Washington New Town was drawn up by Richard Llewelyn-Davies, who was also the man responsible for designing Milton Keynes.

In 1972, renovation began on a derelict farmhouse in the village of Fatfield to transform it into a centre for arts and culture. Originally known as Biddick Farm Arts Centre, the renamed Arts Centre Washington is now home to a theatre, gallery, rehearsal spaces, artist studios and a recording studio.

The 110-seat theatre is now situated in the main barn, whilst the artist studios are in the former cow-shed. Owned by Sunderland City Council, Arts Centre Washington plays host to a wide variety of events, from theatre and music to comedy and dance. In addition, it is home to a range of classes, courses and community activities for people of all ages.

Richard Callaghan

Sunderland's Cultural Journey

WORDS BY *Paul Callaghan*
Sunderland Music, Arts & Culture Trust

Sunderland's Cultural Journey

"proudly claimed to be the biggest ship building town in the world"

Sunderland, like many places in the north and midlands, developed and prospered from the start of the industrial revolution until the second half of the twentieth century. In Sunderland's case, it was coal mining, glass and shipbuilding that provided the jobs and growth upon which the town was built and by the end of the 1930s it proudly claimed to be the 'biggest shipbuilding town in the world', producing a quarter of the UK's tonnage. But the Second World War took its toll with much of the city centre destroyed and then the globalisation of productive industries in the post-war period meant that by the beginning of the 1990s the shipyards, glassworks and mines had all closed and the focus of civic leaders for the next twenty years was much more on the harsh reality of creating new jobs rather than on culture. The cultural renaissance enjoyed by other places such as Gateshead and Newcastle in the late nineties and the noughties was almost seen as an extravagance that

Sunderland could not afford. While its economic prospects began to revive with Nissan, contact centres and the software sector, the city centre fell into a deep recession as both commercial employers and retailers left and by 2010 about a third of city centre properties were empty and in some cases derelict. While there was music in the concert halls of Gateshead and drama in the theatres of Newcastle there was just vertical drinking in the bars and on the street of Sunderland. Yet in back bedrooms and tiny venues people still kept writing and producing music and Sunderland's sculptors, artists and writers continued to work away, often with little recognition.

By the late noughties even Sunderland's prize cultural asset, the National Glass Centre, opened in 1998 as tribute to its lost glass industry, was in serious financial trouble with visitor numbers falling, an expensive facility to maintain and at the time a less than ambitious cultural programme.

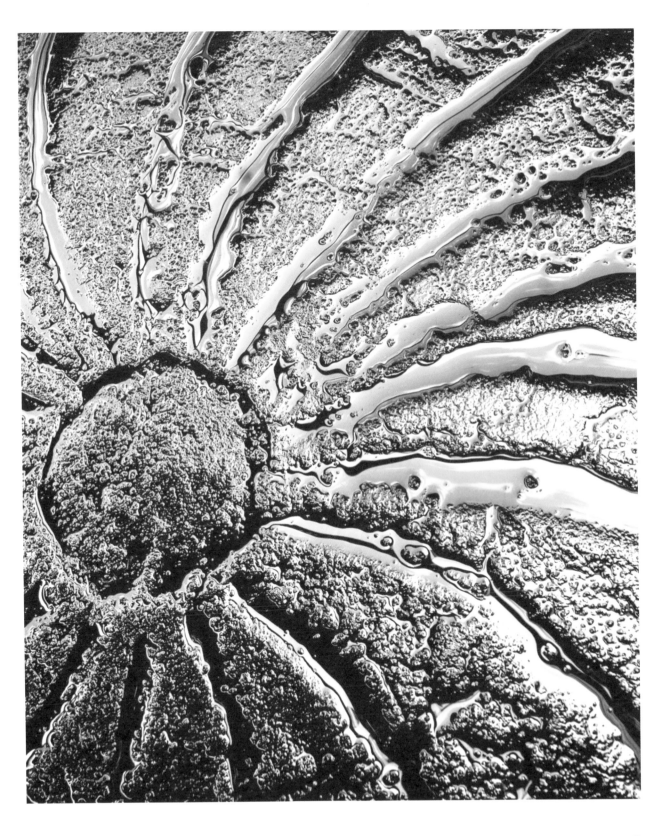

Paul Callaghan

But as the saying goes, sometimes the darkest hour is just before the dawn.

It was at this point in 2010 that Sunderland's fortunes began to change. Sunderland University, with its focus as a civic university, realised the enormous detrimental impact that the imminent closure of the National Glass Centre would have both on the cultural life of the city and on its reputation. As an institution, the University is not rich but has a fierce belief in social mobility and the value of education and a strong attachment to place. The University Board, despite the challenge of taking on such a potentially financially draining asset, agreed to begin the process of negotiating a deal with the Arts Council, the City Council and the then board of the National Glass Centre. This led to the University taking over the NGC in 2010, maintaining it as an independent charity but under the auspices of the University. This was obviously a calculated risk that could have seriously damaged the University's reputation and finances had it failed but the University believed it was a risk worth taking and that decision has subsequently been proved correct. For it was this takeover of the National Glass Centre that began a cultural journey, not just for the University but for the City as a whole – a cultural journey that can be seen in three overlapping periods:

• Formulating the Vision - 2010–2016;
• Assembling the Assets - 2013–2019; and
• Delivering the Dividend - 2021–onwards.

The takeover of the National Glass Centre was to act as a catalyst for other factors that now came into play. One significant factor that should not be underestimated in Sunderland's Cultural Journey has been the increasingly important part that the Council has played in helping to formulate and deliver this vision. For many councils 'culture' is low on the agenda, particularly in times of increasing financial

constraints, yet Sunderland City Council has emphatically committed to this process of cultural regeneration as councillors and officers recognise its benefit both economically and politically. Council backing has come in the form of partnership, asset transfer, funding and most importantly trust and belief in what we are doing.

Other cultural leadership has come from the private sector and the voluntary sector. In 2012, John Mowbray, Chairman of the NorthEast Cultural Partnership, and Paul Callaghan, Chairman of the University, decided that another body, independent of the University and specifically focused on culture, was needed in Sunderland and so formed the Music, Arts and Culture Trust (The MAC Trust) with three main objectives:

• the development of major infrastructure projects for arts and culture or to support arts and culture;
• the delivery, promotion and support of cultural activity, events and cultural organisations;
• the establishment of innovative governance structures in

partnership with key civic players to create and deliver a cultural strategy for the city.

From the beginning the MAC Trust aimed to be a catalyst, developer and promoter of cultural activities within Sunderland, bringing together people with ability, talent and ambition who shared a vision for Sunderland's future as a vibrant, creative and exciting place where the arts, music and culture could flourish and where the city and wider region's culture and heritage could be embraced. The Trust encourages people of all ages and all backgrounds to participate in cultural activities such as playing an instrument, learning to dance, act or sing or creating literature or poetry and to enhance their knowledge and understanding of both culture and heritage. The Trust is also building audiences for arts and cultural performances in Sunderland as well as developing the infrastructure and venues needed for this cultural renaissance in the city.

In 2013 with the support and encouragement of Arts Council England and the Heritage Lottery Fund, the University, the City Council and the MAC Trust came

"The Trust encourages people of all ages and backgrounds to participate in cultural activities... to enhance their knowledge and understanding of both culture and heritage"

together to form the Sunderland Cultural Partnership and in 2014 published an ambitious Cultural Strategy for the City.

Partnering with the MAC Trust and the Customs House, South Shields, in 2013 the University established 'the Cultural Spring', the Arts Council funded, Creative People and Places Programme for Sunderland and South Tyneside that has been operating successfully from 2014 and has recently been extended to the end of 2019.

In 2015 the Council published the 3,6,9 Vision, an ambitious plan to shape the cultural and economic development of Wearside in the coming years. Each year leading up to 2024 was given a specific theme. It began in 2015 with events to mark the 150th anniversary of the publication of Alice in Wonderland, which has strong connections to Sunderland through its author Lewis Carroll. Among the other themes are Sunderland's industrial heritage and future as well as Sunderland AFC's 140th anniversary in 2019. It will culminate in 2024 with a celebration of 1,350 years since the Venerable Bede was born. While it used culture events as its milestones, the plan sought

PLUTUS·RUSSELL·
VESPER·WHITE·
WILLIAM·XI·
1823

AMITY·ARGO·ASIA·
BOREAS·DORIS·HERALD·
HYLTON CASTLE·
KINGSTON·
MALTA·MINA·PHAETON·
PYRAMUS·WILNA
1822

CECRUP·FERRET·FORD·
LADY FRANCES·
LADY LOUISA·NEPOS·
STERS·SYLPH·ZENO
1821

JOHN·JOSEPH·
N·NEREUS·
ULIN

Sunderland's Cultural Journey

to develop the city's infrastructure, economy, skills and vibrancy.

In 2016 the University published its Strategic Plan 2016 - 2021 setting out an ambitious, relevant and clear statement of intent that built on its strengths. Specifically, it describes the University as a place shaper and stressed this in terms of its continued leadership of cultural projects such as Sunderland Culture Ltd and the Cultural Spring, while continuing to enhance iconic cultural venues like the National Glass Centre. The University has also taken a lead role in the bid for Sunderland to be named UK City of Culture 2021. It is the home of the Northern Centre of Photography and the North East Photographic Network and has taken over the Northern Gallery for Contemporary Art from the City Council. And the University is not stopping there, with innovative partnerships with cultural organisations like Live Theatre, Newcastle, to enhance its cultural programmes and ambitious plans for new cultural buildings, new cultural programmes and increased research on the arts and culture.
The takeover of the National Glass Centre was followed

at the Massachusetts Institute of Technology (MIT). His idea was a simple one: to provide the environment, skills, advanced materials and technology to make things cheaply and quickly anywhere in the world, and to make this available on a local basis to entrepreneurs, students, artists, inventors, businesses and in fact, anyone who wants to create something new or bespoke. FabLab Sunderland is part of a global network of digital fabrication spaces that provide 3D printers, laser cutters, vinyl cutters and other facilities and combines a workspace, community maker-space and learning zone – encouraging people to collaborate, exchange ideas and make things happen. As a space for innovation, creativity and collaboration the FabLab links science, technology, engineering, arts and mathematics together and is a place for anyone and everyone who has an idea and wants to make it.

As part of its wider city-centre regeneration programme Sunderland City Council commissioned nationally-renowned Broadbent Studio to create an integrated artwork, celebrating the lives of the workers who created Sunderland's world class shipbuilding industry. As a major piece of public art

"The university has also taken a lead role in the bid for Sunderland to be named UK City of Culture 2021."

by a period of planning, fundraising and then refit and refurbishment leading to a reopening of the building in 2013. The revitalised and refocused National Glass Centre has been a major success, attracting large numbers of visitors, providing world-class facilities as the home base of some wonderful glass artists and an educational experience for not just Sunderland University's students but also for school children and people of all ages who come to learn about glass and how to make glass.

The Music, Arts and Culture Quarter in the Edwardian heart of the city began to take shape from 2014 with the initial grant from the Heritage Lottery Fund and further grant funding from Arts Council England. This development is described in detail elsewhere in this book and also in 2014 one of Sunderland's best known cultural landmarks, Roker Pier, was reopened following extensive renovation work funded by a large grant from the Heritage Lottery Fund.

An important and valuable asset to Sunderland's creative community opened in 2015 with the launch of the University's FabLab. The idea for Fab Labs was conceived by renowned inventor and scientist Professor Neil Gershenfeld

this needed to tell the story of an industry and coincidentally the distance from the city square to the River Wear is almost exactly the length of the Nordic Crusader, at 292m, the longest ship ever built on the river and this wonderful artwork reflects this scale. 'The Propellers of the City' sculpture sits at the end of the granite 'Keel Line' carved with the names of all the ships built on the Wear and illustrated by Sunderland-based graphic novelist and artist, Bryan Talbot. Visitors are able to turn the 3.5m diameter glass and bronze propeller to allow a close inspection of the 500 inlayed photographs of former shipyard workers which were all collected through an active engagement process with them and their families. This interactive element is really important and empowers the audience, as well as helping people find their personal photo within the glass design. Keel Square, the location of the Propellers of the City and the Keel Line was a fitting location in September 2015 for Sunderland to launch its bid to become UK City of Culture 2021. This bid symbolised the cultural ambition that the city now has and the journey that it has travelled since 2010.

Sunderland's Cultural Journey

"Cultural development cannot be achieved without good people leading it."

"...put arts,culture and heritage at the heart of communities delivering real impact in areas across the whole city..."

An important stage in the development of the city's cultural ambitions was the establishment of Sunderland Culture Ltd a new, independent, non-profit making, limited company and charity that was established in 2016 to lead the City's arts and heritage ambitions.

The organisation is a unique strategic and operational organisation formed by the City Council, the University and the MAC Trust to manage the city's key cultural assets. It will also take the lead in bringing new funding to the City to support major projects and will provide strong, strategic leadership to enable Sunderland to realise its cultural ambitions over the next decade.

Through smart and well-connected operational management across a number of central venues, it will enable shared service efficiencies and financial savings whilst also being more adaptive and nimble to meet operational needs. It will provide an appropriate central vehicle for fundraising and income generation for the cultural sector in the city and as an independent registered charity, it will be able to raise money from sources not available to either universities or local authorities.

It will enable joined up communication and marketing initiatives to maximise the visibility of cultural activities and assets in the city both locally and nationally and ensure that communities across the city have opportunities to engage as audiences or participants. Through aggregated capacity it will help create better networks and partnerships nationally and internationally for the city and will provide a strong governance model for major projects such as the UK City of Culture Bid.

As part of the establishment of Sunderland Culture the long-established Northern Gallery of Contemporary Art, which focuses on producing exhibitions of new work by emerging and established regional, national and international artists was transferred from the City Council to University.

One of Sunderland Culture's first successes was winning £1.25m of funding from The Great Place Scheme, jointly funded over three years by Arts Council England and Heritage Lottery Fund, to put arts, culture and heritage at the heart of communities, delivering real impact in areas across the whole city working in partnership with communities and local organisations on initiatives to boost the creative economy, health and well-being, community cohesion and opportunities for young people.

2016 saw a number of other significant cultural achievements. The Dun Cow, the first phase of the Music, Arts and Culture Quarter won national recognition as the country's Best Restored and Best Conserved pub and the Cultural Partnership delivered its first major commissions with Asunder and 10×10.

Commissioned as part of the 14-18 NOW World War 1 Centenary Art Commissions, Asunder explored the legacy of the Battle of the Somme through the prism of a single city – Sunderland. In July 1916, British, French and German forces began one of the most traumatic battles in military history. Over the course of just four months, more than one million soldiers were captured, wounded or killed in the battle, a confrontation of unimaginable horror. Under the creative direction of writer and musician Bob Stanley, Asunder explored its impact on Sunderland. Esther Johnson's film used local archive footage to convey the story of the city's involvement in the First World War, from the men who

Sunderland's Cultural Journey

fought in the fields to those who stayed behind to work in the region's shipyards and munitions factories. The soundtrack to the film was created by two renowned local bands, Sunderland's Field Music and Newcastle's Warm Digits, who performed it live with the Royal Northern Sinfonia at its premiere in the Sunderland Empire. The piece has since gone on to tour the country, playing venues ranging from the Barbican and the Lowry to small community centres and village halls.

In March 2016 Sunderland Cultural Partnership also launched 10x10, an aspirational artist and business initiative and the first strand of 100 Artists into 100 Businesses, part of North East Culture Partnership's regional 15 year Case for Culture. Its aims were innovation and collaboration and while the idea of artists working with businesses is by no means a new one, what was new was the idea that within the North East each place could make a shared commitment to facilitate arts and business cooperation in a way that worked for our own localities' unique challenges and opportunities.

Sunderland Cultural Partnership successfully delivered the first phase of 100x100 in preparation for its delivery throughout the north east region.

Cultural development cannot be achieved without good people leading it and during this period there have been a number of key appointments made: Keith Merrin became Director at National Glass Centre and CEO of Sunderland Culture, Rebecca Ball became the Director of the City of Culture Bid and Helen Green became Director of the Fire Station. Additionally, there were important appointments for the partner organisations in this cultural regeneration: Irene Lucas, Chief Executive and Fiona Brown, Executive Director of People at Sunderland City Council, Shirley Atkinson appointed Vice Chancellor and Professor Michael Young and Steve Knight as DVCs at the University all brought talent and experience to their respective roles but also a shared understanding of how culture could enhance the city and how their organisation could play a role in that process.

Through a broad, balanced and sustainable programme of high quality art and cultural activities for all, the city will create and promote excellent arts and cultural programmes and events that engage and involve participants, encourage new and diverse audiences and enhance the wellbeing of the communities we work with. The objective is that by 2021 Sunderland will be a nationally recognised leader for its joined-up approach to arts and culture through its physical infrastructure with a small number of distinct and vibrant city centre hubs covering live performance, visual arts and heritage with a joined-up offer, complemented by a more dispersed city-wide infrastructure of community venues. It will be important to engage with the people of Wearside through a co-ordinated cultural marketing offer across the city to give everyone the opportunity to participate or be the audience with culture at the heart of addressing the city's challenges and opportunities. The 2020's will see a significant growth in the city's creative industries, artists and cultural production with clear graduate progression routes, more dedicated spaces for creative start-ups and more opportunities for apprenticeships and internships. Importantly Sunderland's reputation as a cultural centre will grow as it is recognised for vibrancy and its large, popular, cultural offer and the city will be seen as a national centre of excellence for glass, photography and contemporary visual arts and as an exporter of cultural brilliance.

"the city will be seen as a national centre of excellence...and as an exporter of cultural brilliance"

Paul Callaghan

International Community Organisation of Sunderland

Established in 2009, the International Community Organisation of Sunderland (ICOS) works to improve the quality of life of the city's BME (Black and Minority Ethnic) communities and improve social cohesion by creating intercultural understanding and building bridges.

The organisation has significant experience and expertise in engaging Eastern European citizens living in Sunderland and the north east, many of whom have limited access to services, benefits, information and support networks due to linguistic, cultural or legal barriers. To do this, ICOS works through a range of targeted projects, including employment and skills, volunteering, access to information and advocacy, as well as diverse cultural projects.

The organisation helps the city's different communities celebrate diversity through projects that lead to intercultural dialogue such as the 'Made in Poland' Festival, that celebrated the achievements of new migrants. The festival included pop-up exhibitions of visual art, cookery sessions, crafts and language tasters and brought established artists together with those just starting their artistic journey. Working in partnership with Sunderland Museum, ICOS organised the 'Meet your Neighbour' project specifically inviting local people to get to know Eastern Europe art and culture including visual art, computer graphics, paintings, photographs and poetry. The organisation is proud of the role it plays in Sunderland, promoting the music, visual art and culture of all of the Eastern European states, from Poland to Hungary and from Slovakia to Lithuania.

As part of Sunderland's 2021 City of Culture bid, ICOS built on this experience to create an exhibition with over twenty Eastern European artists, attracting more than 1500 visitors to its opening weekend in May 2017. It engages local children and young people in activities such as signing folk songs from Poland, Slovakia and Russia and leads Sunderland's 'International Language and Culture Day' supporting the city's journey to become the UK's next Capital of Culture by celebrating the language, culture and food of countries as diverse as China, Poland, Pakistan and Slovakia.

Daniel Krzyszczak

Sunderland Cultural Partnership

WORDS BY *Helen Connify*
Sunderland Cultural
Partnership Coordinator

Sunderland Cultural Partnership

"...The unique relationship between university, city council and business sectors."

Necessity, they say, is the mother of invention.

In 2012 the broader cultural landscape in Sunderland felt like a significantly different prospect to today. While there were clear areas of creative excellence with strong historic legacies, particularly within the University, Northern Gallery for Contemporary Art, independent music and glass sectors, and a strong local connection to heritage, few would argue that the general perception of culture in Sunderland was one of low engagement and a less than dynamic overall offer.

Around this time the University of Sunderland, having recently taken over the leadership of National Glass Centre, and Sunderland City Council, about to establish its own independent museums service, began what would become a productive ongoing conversation with colleagues in Arts Council England, Heritage Lottery Fund and within cultural organisations around the city, to identify the crux of why the city wasn't achieving its creative potential. One area where there was almost unanimous agreement from the outset was that while there were areas of significant expertise, there was

little by way of critical mass and coordination to maximise it.

And so, in 2013 the decision was taken by the University and City Council, to establish a cultural partnership – a mechanism to coordinate conversations, joint planning and most importantly, agree a set of common shared principles and goals that key organisations – those run by Council and University, as well as independent ones – could align to. Sunderland Cultural Partnership formerly came into being in April 2013, with the initial priority to establish a core group with responsibility to drive the creation of a new shared vision for culture in Sunderland. The group was led by University of Sunderland, Sunderland City Council and the Music, Arts and Culture Trust, the business-led arts charity, which was in the early stages of creating ambitious and far reaching plans for a cultural quarter around the development of the old Fire Station, and a consortium partner with both University of Sunderland and Customs House in South Shields, on the Creative People and Places bid to establish the Cultural Spring.

Here in the UK, there were a number of established cultural partnerships we could look to for insights into potential structures and processes that have worked elsewhere and the impact that could be expected; including Manchester Cultural Partnership and Liverpool Arts and Regeneration Consortium in the North West and closer to home Newcastle Gateshead Cultural Venues (NGCV), which provides a strategic umbrella for ten of the biggest cultural organisations on Tyneside.

But there were, from the outset, some marked differences that would set the Cultural Partnership in Sunderland apart from others, most notably the unique relationship between university, city council and business sectors. And whilst Sunderland is a large city in terms of population and geography, its cultural infrastructure is relatively compact, with only one National Portfolio Organisation (at that time for National Glass Centre and Northern Gallery for Contemporary Art), one major commercial theatre venue (Sunderland Empire), the Museum and Winter Gardens, and a range of medium to smaller venues and organisations (including for example Arts Centre Washington and North East Photography Network). Whilst in some respects the prospect of building and expanding that infrastructure was one of the most challenging strategic, long-term ambitions of this new collaboration, and being mindful of how much resource existed within the city to take our ambitions forward, the practicality of managing a smaller number of institutional conversations enabled us to be fairly fleet of foot and responsive to what was working, or not – at all levels.

A seemingly simple proposition therefore on face value; to form a partnership, agree priorities, establish work streams, begin delivery. But the complexity of manoeuvring around

Sunderland Cultural Partnership

many organisational priorities, legacies and ways of working meant finding a careful balance between clarity in approach and communication with a level of flexibility and responsiveness. Either way the first year was a significant learning curve – learning about each other, how we worked, what worked, what didn't work…

We began by hosting a number of exploratory conversations. We brought people together around broad topics; visual arts, performing arts, music, learning and outreach, audience development and heritage. The City Council led the conversations for heritage, based around the work it was doing to establish a new museums service and heritage offer. For the other groups, a common set of questions was the starting point, based around current and future priorities and programmes, assets and facilities, relationships within the city, region and beyond, gaps in provision, barriers to progress and engagement, opportunities and threats on the horizon.

"We brought people together"

People were generous – with their time, their honesty and their commitment to support the process. Some were particular stalwarts, lobbying for the partnership approach. Roll call for colleagues within the Cultural Spring, Arts Centre Washington, North East Photography Network, Northern Gallery for Contemporary Art, National Glass Centre, Sunderland College, Canny Space and Churches Conservation Trust, Sunderland Museums and Heritage Service, Sunderland Libraries, MAC Trust, Sunderland Empire, No Limits Theatre, Artworks North East, Culture Bridge North East and it's precursor Bridge North East, Pop Recs, The Bunker and Independent, plus a raft of individual artists, musicians and local history experts – for an unwavering good spirit and generosity with their thinking.

Some of the early conversations were difficult. Some were productive. Some were brilliant and brought sparks of ideas and energy that became real game changers. In any event, one thing which united every discussion, was a massive commitment from every individual to contribute their absolute best to making things better in this city.

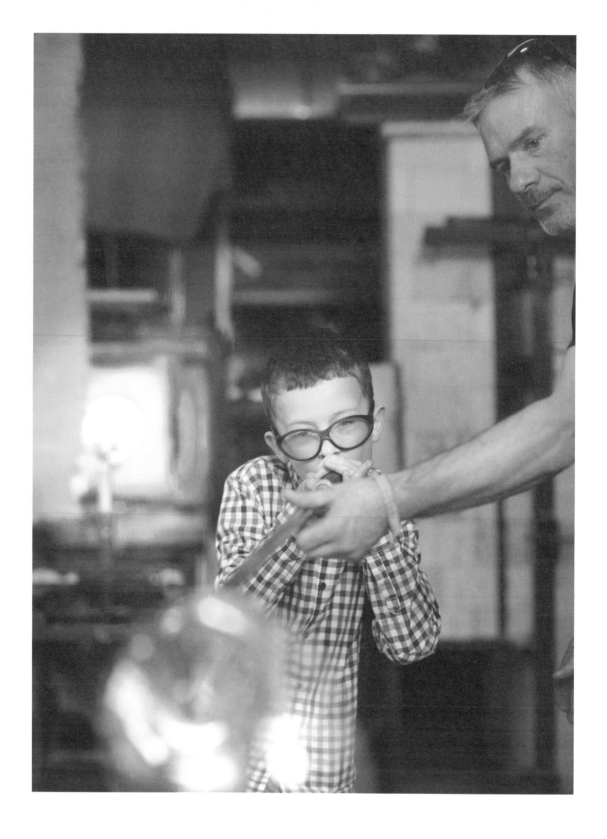

Sunderland Cultural Partnership

And some clear areas began to emerge. The city had a strong historical narrative, but one that was hard to define looking forwards. The "whole experience" of the city felt incomplete and disconnected. The expertise and international reputation of Northern Gallery for Contemporary Art (which pre-dates both MIMA in Middlesbrough and BALTIC Centre for Contemporary Art in Gateshead), National Glass Centre and North East Photography Network were clearly recognised as a strength in contemporary visual arts, glass and photography to build and capitalise on. The performing arts offer in Sunderland was partial, with one very large commercial theatre space regularly attracting audiences in excess of 2000 (Sunderland Empire), a medium-sized one (Arts Centre Washington) and a number of smaller venues. With the exception of The Empire, attracting significant and consistent audiences to performances, events and musical festivals was a challenge. Sunderland had built a community of artists and creative businesses over the years, however a continuing trend saw graduates and successful artists leaving the city for opportunities elsewhere. Support for early and mid-career

independent space for a burgeoning creative community in the city. The critical mass of these moments happening around the same time was a flashpoint and gave insight into how things could be if this level could be sustained. More successes followed. North East Photography Network launched *The Social*, the first international celebration of photography in the North East during October and November, which saw Sunderland as a hub of creative events with photographic work brought out into public spaces, attracting national and international critical acclaim. And later that year Arts Centre Washington launched Sunderland Stages; programming more theatre, dance and spoken word performances into venues, unexpected and hidden spaces across Sunderland.

And then Hull happened; that meteoric rise which came from an ambitious game plan, with the weight of a city behind it. And the question started to be asked 'why not Sunderland?' The time seemed right; as plans came together, investment began and for the first time in a long while, people began to *believe*. Some of us visited our colleagues

"North East Photography Network launched The Social, the first international celebration of photography in the North East"

stage artists to help sustain and develop their practice was patchy. And our ability to leverage significant funding and sustainable models of delivery was limited.

In the midst of these conversations, around summer of 2013, things became interesting -a real head of steam developed when people started to tangibly feel the positive impact of a number of key developments. Firstly the consortium of University of Sunderland, MAC Trust and Customs House was successful in its bid to Arts Council England's Creative People and Places Fund, and were awarded £2m to launch the Cultural Spring. Secondly, National Glass Centre re-opened under the leadership of University of Sunderland, amidst a buzz of national coverage after a £2.3m capital redevelopment. Thirdly, Grayson Perry opened The Vanity of Small Differences in Sunderland Museum and Winter Gardens, attracting record visitors over the summer months. And finally, Pop Recs opened in a disused shop space in the city centre, using the talent, connections and graft of Sunderland band Frankie and the Heartstrings to pull in major music acts and create an

in Hull - who were generous with their time and insights. It further changed the dynamic of conversations and added to the mix another clear target and end game that we could collectively rally towards. Crucially for us though, was the mutual understanding that while we were in it to win it, the process of bidding and committing to delivering that vision was the real prize.

A year after the decision to form a cultural partnership, real progress had been made; we better understood each other's position, ways of working, established our key priorities and what we were going to do to address them.

We agreed we would:
• Help to build confident 'cultural consumers'; improving the way our schools, College and University work together to establish, enhance and sustain cultural opportunities, experiences and confidence for our children and young people.
• Build audiences across the city; identifying audience groups and the intelligence currently held on them, identifying and addressing the barriers to engagement.

• Co-ordinate our messages to present a much clearer picture of what's on offer.

• Keep talent in the city, support it, attract it here and help it flourish.

• Define Sunderland's Unique Selling Proposition around its strengths in glass and photography – particularly in regard to National Glass Centre, Northern Gallery for Contemporary Art, Northern Centre for Photography and North East Photography Network.

• Improve the performing arts offer; support for emerging talent and considering the approach to developing new venue space and using alternative or underutilised spaces.

By October 2014 the partnership was ready to publicly launch its vision for the city, with an initial two-year work plan to begin to address our city's cultural priorities. We hosted a launch event at National Glass Centre to celebrate and invited colleagues from around the North East, with a keynote speech from Sarah Maxfield from Arts Council England, who offered clear words of support and endorsement for the approach and outcomes, particularly flagging up the unique collaboration between University, Council and business as being one which could set a new standard for cities in the future.

"Keep talent in the city"

Bruce Tuckman suggested in 1965, that all successful teams go through distinct stages to become fully functioning and effective. Since October 2014, it's fair to say that those involved in the early stages of delivering the city's cultural regeneration have gone through a phenomenal and rapid period of forming, storming, norming and now onto… performing.

The Cultural Partnership has a leadership group and work stream groups that meet regularly. Work streams currently focus on support for early and mid-career artists, events and joint programming, learning and outreach, audience development and sector resilience. In many ways though, the main success of the partnership approach so far has been to forge dedicated time and space amidst busy diaries and workloads, to talk to colleagues, exchange, find room to grow ideas and thinking, improve and align performance.

Helen Connify

It's not about re-inventing the wheel, taking ownership of output or forcing a direction of travel. The collaborative approach has facilitated much of the current ambitions, plans and success, but the achievement and ownership absolutely is in the hands of each organisation and individual.

There are some landmark projects which have come to fruition recently as a result of the collaboration forums. Asunder is the North East's first co-commission from 1418 NOW; the UK's official arts programme for the First World War centenary. Asunder is the story of the North East home front in 1916, told through largely unknown personal stories in a film using archive and newly filmed footage, from award winning artist and film-maker Esther Johnson, with a new soundtrack scored by Mercury Prize nominees Field Music, and electronic duo Warm Digits, performed live with Royal Northern Sinfonia, creatively produced by musician, author and music journalist Bob Stanley. The event had a major participation programme for communities across the city with community, heritage and arts organisations demonstrating a great capacity to pull local audiences and participants, and find rich pickings for content in the process.

In March 2016 Sunderland Cultural Partnership launched Sunderland 10x10; an aspirational artist and business programme for 2016 and first strand of 100 Artists into 100 Businesses - a key initiative of North East Culture

Partnership's regional 15 year Case for Culture. Sunderland 10x10 had at its heart two core aims: innovation and collaboration. By brokering conversations between local businesses and artists we hoped to create opportunities to develop new, critically engaged work in collaboration for mutual benefit and learning.

We're fortunate here in Sunderland to have great support and dialogue between the cultural and business sectors and we are grateful to our ten business partners for their collaboration: Ashmore Consulting, Arc Adoption (supported by The Cultural Spring), Fab Lab (supported by University of Sunderland), MAC Trust, Northumbrian Water, Sunderland AFC, Sustainable Enterprise Strategies, Siglion Investments and Siglion Developments.

Following a Collaborative Workshop hosted by the project's co-producer Suzy O'Hara, ten selected artists and businesses had one month to work together to develop a proposal which demonstrated creativity and impact to both artist and business. They pitched their proposal to a panel which included two business and three arts experts. Two pairings were awarded commission funds of £7500 to realise their brief which were completed by November 2016. And we are pleased to see that some of the unsuccessful pairings have remained in contact and continued to work together via other means.

"An incredible demonstration of commitment from our colleagues in Sunderland's business sector who have taken a real leap of faith"

Other particular successes include work from the Learning and Outreach Group who have collaborated over the past three years on a new approach to delivering Arts Award, making Sunderland the UK's first Arts Award Supporter City. The key difference sees organisations and art forms delivering different strands of Arts Award together – music in National Glass Centre with glass instruments, theatre with the natural history collection in Sunderland Museum and Winter Gardens, and so on. That group also successfully delivered a ground - breaking 'relaxed' summer programme in the city during 2015. Led by Sunderland Empire's Creative Learning Team and No Limits Theatre, with the National Theatre's Learning Team, a bid to Arts Council England was successful, to create a learning programme for families living with Autistic Spectrum Disorder (ASD), based around the Curious Incident of the Dog in the Night-Time coming to Sunderland Empire during August. Staff in venues around the city including Sunderland Museum, National Glass Centre, NGCA and Arts Centre Washington, took part in ASD training, and collectively devised a programme of activity aimed at ASD families, so that on any day during the summer holidays, there was a cultural activity happening somewhere in the city that was relaxed: an approach that has been embedded into programming. In addition to this Sunderland Empire has been pivotal in developing a new approach to 'supported' performances that have become a benchmark for ATG nationally.

Collectively, these groups worked to build a bid for Sunderland to become UK City of Culture in 2021. It feels like a natural progression and we've done an awful lot to lay the groundwork for it to succeed. There is a raft of other great work and projects too, many resulting from the forum for dialogue with colleagues. Its come from clear leadership, strong delivery, belief in each other, commitment, persistence, negotiation and tenacity on all sides; expertise and excellence at all levels. There's still a long way to go and the city's cultural sector is by no means blind to the scale of the challenge ahead, or the areas where we still need to make ground. But at this point, four years from forming the partnership, the landscape in Sunderland has evolved so much, not only have we delivered the bulk of our initial two year commitments, we're on a track to take the city's cultural offer in directions we didn't think possible in 2013.

Made With Pride

Made in Tyne & Wear is the regional television channel, based in Sunderland, that celebrates the diversity, culture and inimitable style and attitudes of the people who live in this amazing part of the world.

Recognising the impact its content has on the local community, Made in Tyne and Wear is committed to reflecting the lifestyles and tastes of all of its viewers, representing their stories accurately, truthfully and with empathy. The station is particularly delighted to be leading the way with award-recognised LGBT+ programming that is produced locally and broadcast regionally, nationally and internationally from its studios in the heart of Sunderland. Made in Tyne & Wear was also the first British broadcaster to feature same-sex couples competing in a televised dance competition for its 'Made On The Dancefloor' series, with first prize being awarded to a same-sex couple.

The 'Made With Pride' show is broadcast across the network promoting equality and diversity, delivering 'Out and Proud' live LGBT+ content for 90 minutes, twice weekly, from 9.30 pm each Tuesday and Thursday. 'Made With Pride' is also streamed live on Facebook and as a radio programme, reaching a world-wide audience of over 2 million across 84 countries. In 2017 the channel also aired 'Drag Idol' for the first time and the weekday magazine show, 'The Lowdown', features coverage of all the region's Prides, including Sunderland Pride.

The channel has been both nominated for and has won several leading awards in recognition of its achievements in creating entertaining, relevant LGBT+ programming. These awards have endorsed the broadcaster's commitment and belief that LGBT+ content is an important and integral ingredient in its programming schedule. In winning the North East and Border Royal Television Society award in 2017, the partnership between Made with Pride and Pride Radio were singled out as particular key achievements.

Made in Tyne & Wear is extremely proud of the LGBT+ community across its region, and is committed to being a champion of all the fantastic events, groups and activities taking place in the north east.

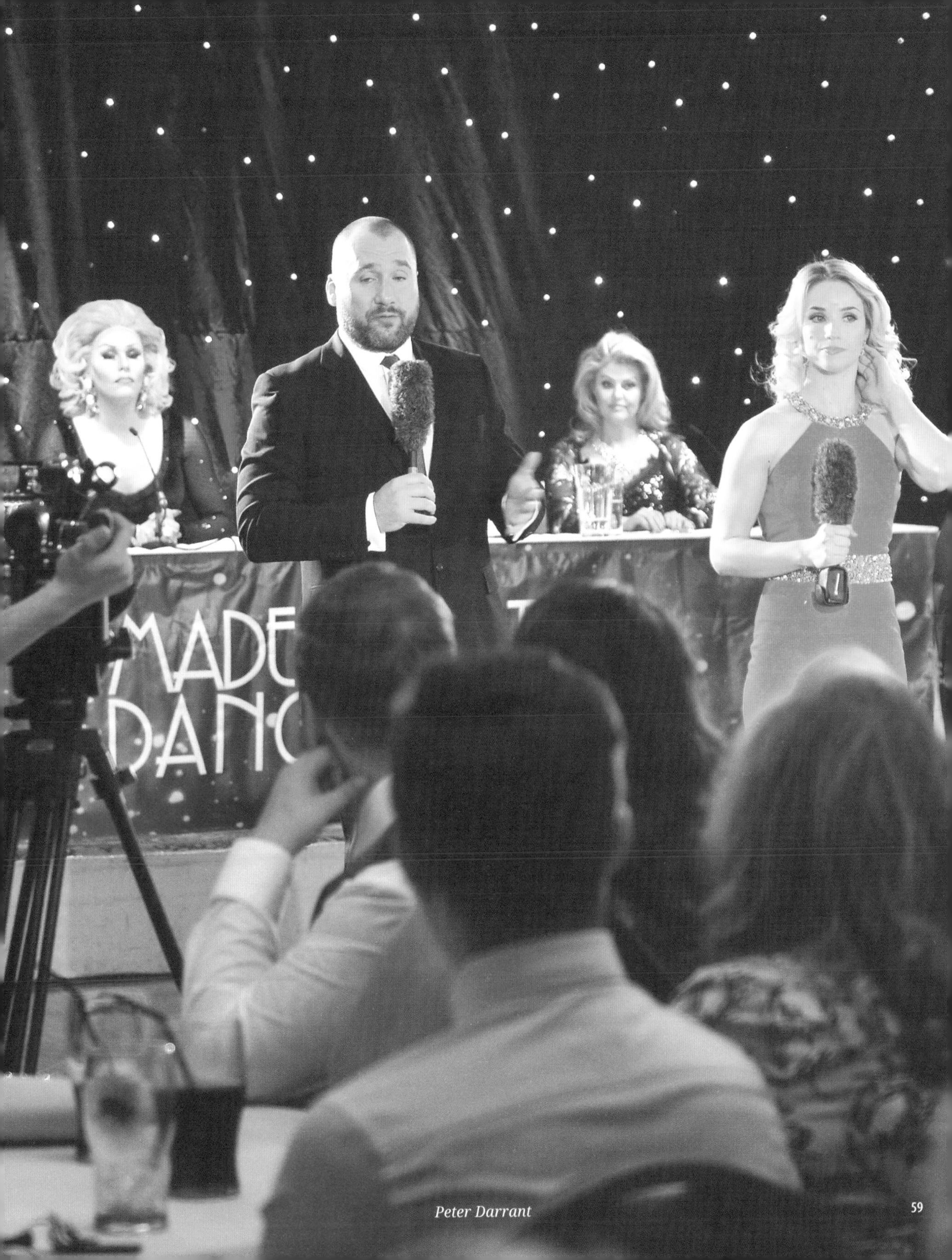

Peter Darrant

The Role of Sunderland's University in Culture

WORDS BY *Graeme Thompson*

Pro Vice Chancellor Connections and
Place, University of Sunderland

The Role of Sunderland's University in Culture

"The city has been a place of higher learning since the 7th Century"

Long before Oxford was making its name as the go-to place for the university elite, there was Sunderland. The city has been a place of higher learning since the 7th Century when Benedict Biscop made it his life's work to build St Peter's Church and Monastery on the north bank of the River Wear. The church – the first in England to have stained glass windows thanks to glaziers brought over from France – still stands proud today. It is the only surviving remnant of the old monastery and overlooks the riverside campus of the University of Sunderland.

This promontory framed by the North Sea at the mouth of the river, was once home to the greatest scriptorium north of the Alps, a collection of books and manuscripts from across the known world, attracting scholars and writers from Rome and beyond. The oldest existing Latin version of the Bible, the Codex Amiatinus, was written at St Peter's. And one of its most distinguished alumni was the Venerable Bede who studied with the monks from the age of seven.

Now, where the scriptorium once existed and the French glaziers fashioned their windows from molten glass, stands a new centre for learning and innovation.

National Glass Centre, a visitor attraction, hot-glass production studio and gallery bringing in more than 200,000 visitors a year, is also home to around 200 staff and students studying glass, ceramics and a highly rated foundation course in Art and Design. Next door is the £12 million media centre named after the university's distinguished former chancellor, film producer Lord David Puttnam.

The young glass artists, journalists and filmmakers studying on the north bank are, in many ways, direct descendants of Bede and those early glaziers. For generations the city has attracted young people wanting to make their mark on the world. Some, like women's rugby captain Katy McLean and Olympic runner Steve Cram, did it through sport and broadcasting; others including Hollywood director Tony Scott and presenter Ortis Deley focused on film and

television; Alison Walker and Josh Halliday went into journalism; Animator Sheila Graber and sculptor Fenwick Lawson became distinguished artists; Jeffrey Campbell (better known as club DJ Assassin) and songwriter Eric Boswell took a music route; Horrible Histories creator Terry Deary and poet Brendan Cleary found fame as writers; Dustan Kitandula and Carl Hagen entered politics; Andrew Zisserman and Tom Hughes-Croucher made their names in science; Chris Svensson and Andy Sandoz took the design world by storm whilst comedian Chris Ramsey and actor Jaz Martin have forged successful careers in entertainment. Like their seventh and eighth Century forebears, today's Sunderland scholars make their presence felt locally, nationally and internationally. Look through the list of university alumni and you'll find thousands of examples of individuals who are now leaders in their field operating across the globe. But the university's biggest impact is undoubtedly on the city of Sunderland itself.

Graeme Thompson

An economic impact survey in 2014 revealed the university generated £561 million for the UK economy and supported more than seven thousand jobs. It produced £200 million for the Sunderland economy and around 4,500 jobs.

Meanwhile its international activities – delivering Sunderland degree programmes in colleges and universities across South East Asia, Africa, Europe and the Caribbean – annually contributes £40 million to the UK's trade balance.

Fifteen thousand students and more than a thousand staff play an important role in the city. Students and academics from overseas who come to Sunderland add to an increasingly diverse cultural landscape. The institution increasingly defines the city every bit as much as early Christian heritage, glass making, shipbuilding and motor manufacturing.

"It is interesting now, looking back over a century, to see how Sunderland's Victorian and Edwardian forefathers recognised the importance of arts and cultural provision."

The university can trace its modern origins back to 1901. Local employers raised £27,800 to create Sunderland Technical College at the Galen Building in Green Terrace. That same year, a School of Art was set up in the Town Hall. It was a boom period in the history of the town. Grand civic and commercial buildings such as the Empire Theatre and Museum and Art Gallery dominated the townscape. Prosperous dwellings appeared on the outskirts to house the architects of Sunderland's successful economy, defined by shipbuilding, mining, railways and glassmaking.

It is interesting now, looking back over a century, to see how Sunderland's Victorian and Edwardian forefathers recognised the importance of arts and cultural provision. At the town hall, classes were running in Fine Art, Painting and Decorating, Stone and Wood Carving, Photography, Millinery and Dressmaking. Even back then there was a strong connection between study and career. Sunderland was the first in England to introduce the 'sandwich course' enabling apprentices to gain higher qualifications whilst working. By 1908, 25 local firms were involved in the scheme.

And these industry-based classes grew rapidly in the town as employers paid fees for many of the students. By 1934, the College of Arts and Crafts had outgrown its city centre base and moved to new accommodation a mile away in Ashburne House. In 1969, the School of Art merged with Sunderland Technical College and the Teacher Training College to become a polytechnic. Sunderland was among the first of the UK's 30 polytechnics and focused on professional and vocational courses. And with a nod to its heritage, the institution became the first in Britain to establish a degree in Glass Design.

By 1980, Sunderland Polytechnic's student body had leapt to 2,294 full-time and sandwich students, and 1,446 part time scholars. Twelve years later, the polytechnic achieved university status and Sunderland was designated a city by order of Her Majesty the Queen.

Today's university is national and international with more than 20,000 students across the globe. In the UK it is based at three campuses in the city centre, St Peter's Riverside and in London's Canary Wharf. Overseas, the university has established a campus in Hong Kong. Academics from Sunderland are currently working across the globe with 16 partner institutions from Vietnam to Trinidad. Not surprisingly its areas of academic expertise relate directly to the history and culture of Sunderland itself. It offers highly rated courses in creative and cultural industries, teacher education, pharmacy and health sciences as well as advanced manufacturing, engineering, enterprise, business, social sciences, software and sport.

The Role of Sunderland's University in Culture

The university's reputation in arts, design, journalism and media is recognised at home and overseas thanks to its staff, alumni and impressive facilities. Over the past ten years, the institution has made significant investments in cultural and creative education including the Northern Gallery for Contemporary Art, the Northern Centre of Photography, Sunderland Software City, the FabLab, the David Puttnam Media Centre, the award-winning Spark FM, the MediaHub, Priestman Fine Art & Performance studios, the National Glass Centre. and the newly opened Industry Centre and Hope Street Xchange – which provides start-up support for creative graduates. In 2009, the university successfully campaigned for creative industries and culture to be included as a priority in the city's new Economic Masterplan to reflect the impact of the university's reputation on an area of activity that has become the fastest-growing sector of the UK economy. According to figures released in 2016 by the Department of Culture, Media and Sport (DCMS) cultural and creative industries are booming. More than two million people are now employed in a sector worth £87.4 billion and growing at a rate of 9% a year. The North East, and Sunderland in particular, lag behind other parts of the UK when it comes to the number of creative economy jobs as a proportion of total regional employment.

Measures to close that gap and ramp up Sunderland's potential as a creative and cultural centre were outlined in the city's Cultural Strategy, published in the autumn of 2014. The University and City Council were the principal authors of a document which details a fifteen-year plan to re-shape the cultural landscape.

The strategy aims to raise the profile of the city as a cultural destination, nurture creativity and develop audiences and venues. The University believes that a richer cultural offer will not just make the city a more attractive place for students and staff, but also address the issue of talented creative graduates feeling they must move from the area to kick-start their careers.

It is not the first time the University has intervened to make things happen in the city. It was a founding partner in the creation of Sunderland Software City – a European project to set up hundreds of software companies in the area. And it was also the driving force in establishing a centre for advanced manufacturing closely linked to Sunderland's giant Nissan car factory. And of course, it stepped in to redevelop and refresh National Glass Centre.

On the arts and culture agenda, the University, led by its then-president, Professor Peter Fidler, and new vice chancellor, Shirley Atkinson, realised a step-change was needed. The institution was instrumental in the setting up of both the North East Cultural Partnership and the Sunderland Cultural Partnership. Both networks have been key to positioning culture at the heart of the region's revival from post-industrial decline to a globally competitive high skill economy.

The Role of Sunderland's University in Culture

The dynamic chief executive of Arts Council England, Darren Henley, has described the University of Sunderland as "one of a new generation of place-makers" – acknowledging that cultural ambition can make life better for those living and working in the locality. The theme was also picked up by the arts council's then chair, Sir Peter Bazalgette, when he visited the city in February 2016 to give a public lecture on the role of arts in regeneration. He described the university's partnership with Sunderland City Council and the Sunderland Music Arts and Culture Trust as "a poster child" for the way in which culture can reshape an economy.

They both went onto highlight Sunderland and the contribution of its university in their evidence to the Government's Culture Media and Sport committee in May 2016.

The University believes its investment in assets, including National Glass Centre, the David Puttnam Media Centre and the Sunderland Cultural Partnership, enables it to play a pivotal leadership role in shaping policy and strategy for the city. Creating and investing in a new infrastructure to deliver high quality creative and cultural degree programmes has a direct impact on the student experience and the reputation of our graduates. In 2016, Sunderland was the only British university listed as a partner in the UK's 14-18 NOW, the official arts programme for the First World War centenary. The university and the Sunderland Cultural Partnership staged an event titled Asunder – a production to mark in film, archive and music the 100th anniversary of the Battle of the Somme. Sunderland is also the first British university leading a project for Arts Council England's transformative Creative People and Places initiative.

The Role of Sunderland's University in Culture

The Cultural Spring was established in 2013 with a £2m grant to connect hard to reach communities in the North East with artists, performers, writers and musicians. The university's partners in the project are the Customs House in South Shields, Sangini and the MAC Trust. Meanwhile politicians and creative professionals from Gothenburg in Sweden have been to Sunderland to learn more about the work of the university and the Cultural Spring. Their intention is to replicate the project in the west of Sweden.

At the end of 2016 the University transferred from the city council the iconic Northern Gallery for Contemporary Art. Curators from the gallery will contribute to arts provision across the campus. Meanwhile, the University is preparing to move the NGCA into £375,000 new galleries on the ground floor of the National Glass Centre by February 2018. This commitment to cultural development in the city has resulted in the University establishing with the MAC Trust and the city council a new culture company for Sunderland. The company – Sunderland Culture – has

so many of the artists, producers and designers based at the university, Sunderland's Professor of Fine Art, the distinguished sculptor, Eric Bainbridge, involves students in many of his shows here in the UK and overseas.

Then there are the shows by the students themselves. Once a year in early summer, graduating students take over galleries at National Glass Centre, Priestman Building and Cityspace to showcase work in glass and ceramics, photography, fine art, illustration, fashion, animation and design.

It's always a glorious showcase of emerging talent and the shows attract thousands of visitors – including potential employers, commissioners and canny locals who choose to invest in the art of graduates who may one day be as rich and famous as Grayson Perry and Tracey Emin.

University student and Spark FM presenter, Jordan North, has been named as one of four new presenters on BBC Radio One and students regularly secure placements and work experience at leading agencies, publishers and broadcasters. The university has an enviable record in the

> "The university has been at the forefront of research into the ways in which today's artists, performers and producers earn their living. "

recruited five independent trustees to sit alongside board members appointed by the three founding partners. The aim of the company is to manage and develop the city's growing cultural portfolio and is another example of the innovative approach being taken by the university and its partners.

These investments and connections are not just about placemaking. They provide unique opportunities for staff and students to engage in projects and commissions that help shape and enrich the curriculum and the community. Examples include the students working with photographer Julian Germain on a project about loss for the Cultural Spring's Great North Passion on BBC One in 2014; performing arts and music students producing a new choral piece for the same show with composer Will Todd and Graeme Danby of English National Opera; glass students led by academic James Maskrey working with the artist Magdalene Odundo on the spectacular Transitions installation at the National Glass Centre. Staff and students from Fine Art frequently collaborate with curators from the Northern Gallery of Contemporary Art. And like

teaching of journalism and media production. It also has a team of world-leading media academic researchers led by Professors Julia Knight, Trish Winter, Clarissa Smith and Shaun Moores.

There's a trophy cabinet in the foyer of the David Puttnam Media Centre groaning under the weight of awards for student achievement in radio, television and film. The trophies come from the UK – such as the Royal Television Society and the National Student Radio Awards – as well as overseas. For example, students have picked up awards at the New York Festival and in European competitions. At the same time, music, drama, dance and performing arts students are staging performances around the city and at The Sage, Gateshead where the university offers innovative degrees in Popular Music and Jazz and in Community Music. The university has been at the forefront of research into the ways in which today's artists, performers and producers earn their living. An example is its work with the Paul Hamlyn Foundation to recognise that an increasing

number of arts professionals generate most of their income from participatory settings such as charities, prisons, schools and community initiatives.

This has been incorporated into the Sunderland curriculum that emphasises preparation for careers in all of its practice-led degree programmes. In addition, the Faculty of Arts and Creative Industries is developing a Masters programme in Participatory Arts as well as a MOOC (a massive open online course). At a time when students are questioning the value of university degrees because of the government's fees regime, institutions like Sunderland are making more of their graduate success stories. This is particularly the case in the area of arts, culture and humanities in the wake of the current government's policy of encouraging children and parents to focus on science, technology and maths.

The policy has seen many schools drop provision in subjects such as dance, drama, music, arts and crafts. And there are currently no arts subjects included in the new English Baccalaureate.

So the experiences of Sunderland alumni enjoying successful careers in the arts and creative industries have never been more relevant.

There are of plenty of examples; Journalism graduate Josh Hollis completed the BBC Journalism Trainee scheme and is now working as a Social Media Producer for the BBC News Business Unit.

Michelle Collins and Sally Leach both graduated from Advertising and Design and have landed jobs at Saatchi in London.

Media Production graduate Jonny Scrafton is a researcher with Love Productions and has worked on a range of shows including The Great British Bakeoff and Strictly Come Dancing. He's also the recipient of two Royal Television Society Student Awards.

Journalism graduate Ganesh Rau achieved a First at Sunderland and was immediately snapped up to be an Output Producer at Sky News in London.

Carley Armstrong is an inspiring example of the mission to enable students from households with no experience of university to pursue a degree. Carley was a mature student and single parent who completed a range of summer jobs and placements alongside her studies in Media Production. She's now a script supervisor on CBBC's long running drama The Dumping Ground, filmed in the North East. Also staying closer to home is Fine Art graduate Stephanie Goldsmith who now works as a Gallery Learning Facilitator at National Glass Centre.

"The University also recognises that many graduates will end up in freelance careers so it offers business and enterprise skills"

Of course, not all graduates end up working in the UK. Paul Mann from Ashington studied Advertising and Design at Sunderland and is now based in New York with the creative agency Anomaly.

These stories perfectly illustrate the university's life changing philosophy. A new five year strategy also recognizes the changing Higher Education landscape which is now more competitive and challenging than at any other time in its history. Student recruitment has become a free for all with institutions able to enrol as many home and EU scholars as they can take. That's because they increasingly rely on student fees as their main source of income. In the past another major contributor was international recruitment. But in recent years, tough visa restrictions on overseas students able to enter the UK to study, has led to a slump in the number of applicants, who choose instead to enrol with universities outside the UK. In response to

the changing higher education economy, Sunderland plans to maintain at its core the genuine partnership between students and staff, and places at its heart the knowledge creation, research, and learning and teaching expertise of its community of scholars. It acknowledges a world where flexibility and adaptability will be vital indicators of future success. And it recognises the university's moral and financial responsibility to provide an exceptional personalised experience to fee-paying students. That experience offers opportunities to access work integrated and relevant learning through strong engagement with employers and sector leaders.

The academic offer will be increasingly interdisciplinary with a focus on skills in leadership, design, enterprise, digital technologies and innovation. Pharmacy students will be offered the chance to learn about social media marketing and engineers will be introduced to design. These are vital attributes for future graduates as they launch themselves into an always-connected world where technology has blurred the boundaries of work.

In the cultural and creative sector, the University also recognises that many graduates will end up in freelance careers so it offers business and enterprise skills alongside regular workshops and masterclasses from visiting professional artists, producers and designers.

Conversely, the University's cultural offer aims to engage students from all disciplines. Scientists join the University choir, trainee teachers get to broadcast on student radio, business students support the annual film festival and engineers volunteer at National Glass Centre. The days when subjects were locked in silos behind impermeable university walls are no more. Which is good news for a changing University in a changing city.

The University's commitment to culture and the creative industries comes at a time when there are significant barriers to growth. Over recent years, councils in the north of England have been subjected to a continuing series of brutal cuts to public services and there is at the heart of government, a growing appetite for greater measurable benefits from

investment in the arts and higher education. Against this background, the University has stepped up momentum around its role as a placemaker, working with partners from public, private, non-profit, and community sectors to strategically shape the physical and social character of Sunderland and the wider region. There is growing evidence that arts and cultural outreach strengthens communities and impacts on well-being and social cohesion. Researchers at the University are using examples from Sunderland to reinforce the knowledge and understanding around interventions in community access to arts, performance and cultural activity. Staff and governors are fully signed up to the belief that creative placemaking not only animates public and private spaces, rejuvenates structures and cityscapes and improves local business viability, but also brings people together to celebrate, inspire, and be inspired. People who work here, study here and live here. It is a philosophy which dates back to the Venerable Bede who summed it up when he wrote the words Scientiam Dulce Hauriens. The translation from the Latin is Sweetly Absorbing Knowledge. A fitting motto for a university on Bede's doorstep.

Sunderland's Amazing Outdoor Attractions

Sunderland International Airshow

The biggest free annual airshow in Europe, Sunderland International Airshow takes place over three days every July, attracting more than 1,000,000 visitors to the event. It takes place at Roker and Seaburn, and includes stalls and food traders to complement the aerial entertainment.

Originally staged in 1989 as a one-day, one-off event, Sunderland Airshow attracted an unexpected 250,000 people which led to its continuation in subsequent years. The event was extended to two days in 1991, and then to its current three-day format, with festivities stretching from Friday to Sunday of the last weekend in July.

The beautiful beaches provide a wonderful vantage point and the coastline is a superb setting in which to see the aircraft displays over the sea with the pier and lighthouse at Roker forming a fantastic backdrop. Historic military aircraft and high-speed jets are some of the star attractions. It is a great day out for the whole family, with lots of fairground rides and stalls as well as the aircraft displays. Without a doubt, the most popular annual attraction of the show is the Red Arrows Royal Air Force aerobatic team. The nine Hawk T1A planes with their beautiful red, white and blue smoke trails are the grand finale of the air show, and surely one of the most photographed events in Sunderland. Other displays include the Eurofighter Typhoon, the Black Cats, the Royal Navy's helicopter display team, as well as the RAF Falcons parachute display team.

Sunderland's Outdoor Attractions

Sunderland Illuminations

Roker and Seaburn first saw an illuminations festival in 1936, when the lights were confined to Roker Park, with trams along the sea front also decorated. The outbreak of the Second World War and the introduction of mandatory blackouts against aerial bombing brought an end to the illuminations, with the festival not returning to the town until 1949.

The Illuminations ran again until 1959, when they were scrapped, returning to Roker and Seaburn for a period during the 1980s and 1990s. Sunderland Illuminations were brought back for a third time in 2012, and demonstrably still maintain their lustre with Sunderland's crowds as they continue to attract bumper audiences to participate in the light festival which takes place every autumn.

Running from the end of September to the beginning of November, Sunderland Illuminations remains one of the most popular and well attended cultural events in the city, attracting visitors from around the North East to participate in the festivities.

Richard Callaghan

Houghton Feast

A traditional celebration in the town of Houghton-le-Spring, Houghton Feast's history stretches back to the twelfth century, and has its origins in the Michaelmas celebration of the dedication of the church of St Michael and All Angels in Houghton-le-Spring. Bernard Gilpin's appointment as Rector of Houghton-le-Spring saw an expansion of the Feast, with the roasting of a hog or ox every Sunday between Michaelmas and Easter.

Over the years, Houghton Feast has featured a wide variety of events and attractions. Horse racing once played a major role in the Feast, with the last race being held in 1938. During the 1830s, famous entertainer and showman, Billy Purvis, brought a performing bear with him to the Feast.

Houghton Feast was not universally popular. During the 1830s, Methodists held counter-events to try and convince people not to participate in the extravagances and debaucheries of the Feast. The Feast continued throughout both First and Second World Wars, although on a more limited basis than before.

Today, Houghton Feast remains a key event in Houghton's calendar, with festivities taking place every October. The whole community is involved in a programme of events that varies from fireworks and fairground rides to the traditional ox roasting.

The 2018 Tall Ships Race

In July 2018, the Tall Ships fleet will create a stunning spectacle on the banks of the River Wear and within the Port of Sunderland. The event will take place from Wednesday 11th July to Saturday 14th July with numerous activities and attractions around the city, absorbing visitors in a festival of culture that celebrates both the city's maritime heritage and cultural renaissance. The event will include the upbeat Crew Parade, intended to thank the host port for their hospitality, through the city from the Port, bringing a true international carnival atmosphere to the streets. Then, at the end the weekend, the race begins as the ships undock and move out into the North Sea in a stunning Parade of Sail.

"the Tall Ships fleet will create a stunning spectacle on the banks of the River Wear and within the Port of Sunderland."

Richard Callaghan

Regional Partnerships and the Case for Culture

WORDS BY *JOHN MOWBRAY*

Chairman of the North East
Cultural Partnership.

Regional Partnerships and the Case for Culture

"I can see your head is in the region, but your heart is in the city"

"I can see your head is in the region, but your heart is in the city" is the best and most appropriate description of many people who strive to improve their area and one of the nicest things anyone has said about me and others who are working in Sunderland. For all the passion that might surround a city and your belief that you can do things differently, you still need that wider view on things, that support and encouragement from others and that learning and experience from elsewhere. Sometimes it comes from far away or an experience you've had or someone tells you about something new and different or you just copy something that works. If you're developing the cultural offer in any city, you need the mechanisms to learn. The North East of England has a great cultural past going way back to its Roman and Christian heritage and onto to a more sophisticated art and heritage offer today - it is also renowned for its sense of community, identity and its ability to work together. In recent times regional organisations like Northern Arts, The Sponsors Club for Arts and Business, One North East and other organisations acted as the catalyst for development backed by ambitious local authorities who saw culture as a lever for regeneration, participation, wellbeing, economic benefit and promotion. The Case for Capital was produced in the mid 1990's by Northern Arts as an ambitious plan of what could be achieved in the North East with a bit of investment (some £200 million) and some real creativity and imagination. It was launched by Prime Minister to be, Tony Blair, in 1995 and reaching for the moon, it got the stars too as all of the exciting things it talked about happened and a region moved on significantly but one area in particular, Newcastle and Gateshead, were transformed. Here we saw in Gateshead alone the arrival of the Angel of the North, Baltic Contemporary Art Gallery, Sage Gateshead and the Gateshead Millennium Bridge.

Over a decade, these catalyst organisations disappeared and were not initially replaced. The success stories of that time remained but could they be built on? Two examples show what happened. Newcastle and Gateshead came together as two local authorities to establish NewcastleGateshead Initiative essentially as a Destination Marketing Agency. Alongside that, both councils embarked on cultural development, particularly Gateshead, with the iconic buildings and installations listed above, backed by national and local organisations. It was a catalyst for change and theatres and galleries thrived, hotels were built and the visitor economy grew from virtually nothing to £1.2 billion in less than 20 years. In terms of arts and heritage, it has a 365 day cultural offer with over £250 million of world-class facilities. It now has an international reputation for culture, hosting the World Summit on Arts and Culture in 2006 and is seen as one of the leading regions in Europe for public art. It has been voted top city break destination in England, is a Lonely Planet Guide top 30 recommendation, has had nearly 50% increase hotel rooms since 2002 and the highest city hotel occupancy out of London.

The failed bid for European Capital of Culture in 2008 by NewcastleGateshead, led to an unprecedented programme of cultural investment of nearly £50 million across the region led by One North East funding. The Culture 10 programme ensured a plethora of cultural activity and kick-started much activity which helped promote the region and also stimulate its residents.

Rural areas were not neglected in any of this and further up the Tyne Valley at Kielder, the social and economic life was improved but again a partnership started the regeneration. The Kielder Partnership consisted of the Forestry Commission, Northumbrian Water, Northumberland County Council, Calvert Trust and the Environment Agency amongst others. Again supported by a regional body, One North East and a national one, Arts Council England, it used art and culture as its base to build. A sculpture trail around the 26 miles of the reservoir in Kielder Water and Forest Park supported by structures created by world leading artists such as James Turrell started the change. The creation of an observatory helped the area to receive the UK's only Dark Sky status. The UK's most beautiful marathon attracts thousands every year.

John Mowbray

Regional Partnerships and the Case for Culture

Winter Wonderland, organised by Northumbrian Water at Leaplish brings thousands to the area at a time which was traditionally quiet. They work with local cultural organisations such as Dodgy Clutch to bring the event to life. As a result, businesses have been established and visitors have multiplied. The number of direct jobs created in that area has risen by 31% with a similar increase in indirect jobs. The number of visitors to the area has increased by 53% to nearly 400,000 per year over a five year period and 60% of these come from outside of the region. Direct and indirect spend have both risen by 44% to over £22 million in that period.

So partnership at a local and regional level is important but Government policy from 2010 was to break up regions and the organisations that served them. The Government Office of the North East was closed and the Regional Development Agency, One North East, was wound up. Two Local Enterprise Partnerships were set up in the area but with no cultural remit. The Association of North East Councils (ANEC), representing the twelve local authorities, was the only public sector regional organisation remaining although even that has recently been scaled back. The offices and remit of other funders were also reduced. The Government saw no reason for partnerships as they existed and replaced them with poorly resourced economic bodies, ironically called partnerships! Interestingly, business organisations still span the full north east region as partnerships.

ANEC consulted widely in 2011/12 and recognised the need for partnership across the region to prevent the loss of the momentum that had been built up and to build on the success to date. The North East Culture Partnership (NECP) was set up in 2013 in response with minimal funding from each of the twelve local authorities. A board with an independent business co chair and a local authority co chair

Regional Partnerships and the Case for Culture

"This £3 million programme will help them research and develop creative industries. By doing this they will create the right environment and framework for our students to stay and build their businesses in our region"

was set up with representatives of the twelve local authorities, five universities, cultural organisations and business. Two part time project managers were appointed to run the partnership and it was launched to much acclaim in Durham Castle. Initially it focussed on the things which the region was good at and subgroups of experts looked at developing the vision, the universities working together, business and artists working together and developing and sharing the festival and events programme. Local areas established their own cultural partnerships to feed into the region. Sunderland Cultural Partnership was set up in response to this and the need to catch up with other areas-another advantage of regional partnership, watching others and feeling the need to do better. Perhaps that was part of the catalyst for the city. Arts Council, the University and the Council acted together to move from a very low cultural profile to producing their own vision for the city, which was seen as a template for others to follow. The change has been remarkable!

NECP developed in a number of areas. For the first time, the five Universities in the region worked closely together around one issue. They recognised the strength of each of their creative and cultural courses and programmes and the variety that the region offered. Suddenly by acting as a group in a region rather than as individuals in a city, they could cover every eventuality and attract students to the region. They went further by developing Creative Fuse supported by funding from The Arts and Humanities Research Council (AHRC). This £3 million programme will help them research and develop creative industries. By doing this, they will create the right environment and framework for our students to stay and build their businesses in our region.

Festivals and events have been key strengths for the north east and NECP recognised this and the need to ensure a more than adequate communication across the area about what was going on. The Stockton International Riverside Festival has been running successfully for 27 years and continues to attract the best artists in the world. NECP wants it and others to continue but can artists appearing in Stockton perform in Berwick in the next week and vice versa. As well as sharing artists around the area, the intent was to create new opportunities, new festivals and new events. In 2015, Hillfolk Noir from Boise, Idaho, appeared at the well established Sage Gateshead Americana Festival but the next day appeared in the Cultural Spring's Summer Streets Festival in Thompson Park in Sunderland. The sharing was new and a huge success - the first time many attending would have seen an American never mind one playing hillbilly blues!

NECP has also started to look at two other areas. The first around Christian Heritage needs development but recognises (again) the strength of looking at the offer as a region rather than individually. Sunderland and Jarrow have St Peters and St Pauls with the Venerable Bede and St Benedict Biscop, Durham has St Cuthbert (and Bede), Northumberland has Holy Island and of course, there's much more in between. Again connectivity is the key. Connecting to the world is a strength of a region versus an individual. NECP surveyed arts and heritage organisations and found that they work with 61 countries, one third of the world's countries. Partnerships are being developed with the West of Sweden and the Ruhr Region of Germany, but in addition to those which exist especially through twinning arrangements.

The prime piece of work by NECP was a 'homage' to the Case for Capital. In 2015, it produced its Case for Culture. This was positive statement of ambition for 15 years to 2030 demonstrating how culture can play a pivotal role in reinvigorating a place and creating social and economic benefits for the people, who live, work and visit there, building social inclusion and creating a sense of pride in the North East. There are five aspirations in the Case for Culture which apply to cities as well as regions as follows:

1. Participation and reach - spreading the benefits of arts and heritage further to make sure everyone benefits with a target of reaching an extra half a million people every year

2. Children and young people - ensuring we continue to innovate and broaden access to culture for children and young people, for all the benefits this brings to future generations with a target of extending the reach to 285,000 children and young people per year

3. Talent and progression - ensuring we attract and retain the very best cultural and creative talent, and provide routes for career progression to grow a more skilled and diverse workforce

4. Economic value - harnessing our potential to support economic growth and job creation, and attract more visitors to our region with a view to doubling the number of jobs in the creative sector

5. Distinctiveness and innovation - creating a vibrant and distinctive region with an excellent quality of life - the right conditions for innovation and investment

The case also included an investment target of £300 million over 15 years with £100 million already in place.

The Case for Culture was an important document and the references above are virtually word for word. The Culture Minister called it a template for the UK and the partnership as a unique example of working together which he wants every area to repeat. Significant reference was also made to it in the Governments Culture White Paper.

So why is all the regional stuff important? Sunderland cannot stand alone. It has its own culture and heritage, new and old but it can learn from others and the fact that so many things have worked elsewhere in our region means that others will support Sunderland when it tries to do things. From my point of view, I couldn't co chair something like this if it

couldn't benefit my city! I look back at my cultural background and there's not a lot there apart from a belief that art, culture and heritage, done properly can change people's lives - and I've had some involvement in programmes to do exactly that. I've also seen it in cities around the world and I've seen it in the workplace. So my head is definitely in the region but my heart is absolutely in the city.

"The case for Culture...
a template for the UK..."

John Mowbray

Sangini

"Women are at the centre of our work because we believe that when you educate the woman, you educate the family." Sreelekha Reddy, Founder of Sangini

Sangini is a Hindi word meaning 'a friend'. The organisation is a minority-led, multi-cultural women's group that began as a small group of women who met monthly in each other's homes to combat feelings of isolation. They never dreamt that one day they would be transforming the lives of strangers. The group, predominantly from Sunderland, shared their life stories, their concerns, their feelings and their hopes around a table laden with Indian food. Those who had cars made sure that the others got home safely.

"From the outset, inclusion was important." Dr. Gitika Banerjee, Board member and ex-Tyne & Wear Sherriff.

It was formally set up in 2002 with the vision to improve the quality of women's lives by increasing their physical, mental and spiritual health, through artistic, educational, cultural and recreational activities which also celebrate cultural diversity. And in doing so, increase their participation in both civil and civic roles

Sangini's work is informed by its strategic objectives:

• At an Individual level – providing emotional and practical support and encouragement to remove thesocial and cultural barriers for BME women and currently excluded women

• At a Community level – challenge all forms of inequalities, prejudice and discrimination through training and education

• At an Organisational level – promoting our values and sharing resources and best practice through the development of partnerships and joint projects at a local and regional level.

• At a Policy level – engaging with, advocating and influencing local, regional and national policies and strategies.

Sangini has pioneered the arts and culture as a medium to get its well-being message across, and has successfully delivered programmes of what may be termed as 'change management' for women from diverse cultural backgrounds experiencing isolation and mental health issues. For example, one of Sangini's first projects 'Sehat' (meaning health) had a profound impact on the lives of 20 isolated, diverse young women, resulting in a body of art work exhibited at the Sunderland Museum and Winter Gardens.

Sangini plays a crucial role in developing a sustainable infrastructure for social cohesion through promotion, participation and education. Hence, as well as arts projects, Sangini's activitiesinclude: participatory workshops, audience development,

Sangini

advice and guidance, artists' residencies and organising cultural events, such as Diwali – Sunderland Festival of Light and the International Women's Day.

Whilst projects such as Shakti helped to raise awareness about issues of domestic violence within the BME women through visual arts exhibition, poetry and drama, the heritage project 'Stories from our Sisters in Sunderland' captured the life stories of migration and the settlement of women from diverse cultures who made Sunderland their home.

"Projects like the Stories from our Sisters in Sunderland provide us with an opportunity to open up new conversations about the issues related to migration, explore the role of women in maintaining one's cultural identity and acknowledge the efforts made throughout the years in sustaining a stable social infrastructure within the migrant communities." Margaret Dobson, Co-Chair.

Over the past 15 years Sangini has worked with well over 5,000 children and 2,000 women from different communities through a wide range of projects, events and initiatives involving valuable partners from statutory, voluntary and public sector, especially the schools, the arts organisations, museums and galleries.

Currently, Sangini is working with The Cultural Spring as a partner to help widen arts engagement through participatory activities at grassroots level. It has helped to set up a women's art group SWAG (Sunderland Women's Art Group) that meets at C.H.A.N.C.E Community Centre every week. Sangini is also providing support to an artists' group Creative Women's Collective that makes site-specific work using experimental

collaborative approach with the purpose to provide a platform for female artists and increase arts participation among women and girls in the region.

To date, Sangini has built a reputation for inclusivity, creativity

and integrity. It aims to continue inspiring individuals and groups to help generate own narratives through creative expression, that in itself is a vehicle for empowerment and sustainable development.

What Makes Sunderland A 'City Of Culture'?

WORDS BY *REBECCA BALL*
Director, Sunderland 2021

What makes Sunderland a 'City of Culture'?

"Sunderland is an enchanting city. It is a city packed with fascinating stories"

What makes Sunderland, or for that matter any city 'a City of Culture'? Since taking up the role of Director of Sunderland's bid to be UK City of Culture 2021 in February 2016, this is a question that I have contemplated pretty much every day.

Sunderland is an enchanting city. It is a city packed with fascinating stories of cultural significance - a history of glass making which dates back to the 7th Century, a world-renowned shipbuilding heritage, an extraordinary coastal landscape – there is so much that is captivating about the place. Yet it is also a city that has not seen the investment in its arts and cultural fabric that many of its similarly sized peers and neighbours have enjoyed. As such it is easy to become focussed on what is not there, the buildings that a need building, the facilities that need developing, the partnerships that need forming.

All these things are of course vitally important – and thankfully in Sunderland at the moment there are a lot of brilliant people working to make change in this field - but for me the question of what makes a city a City of Culture has a deceptively simple answer. It is the people who live and work there. Maybe the question should be rephrased as 'who' rather than 'what' makes a city of culture.

City of Culture is the opportunity to highlight the distinctiveness, talents, ambitions and stories of a city's people. The city's residents should be the programme's heartbeat; they are its principle stakeholder, its principle agent of its development and should be the principle beneficiary of what is created. The word city derives from civis meaning citizen. The essence of the city of Sunderland is definitely found in its people.

Less than five years ago, however, the UK's national survey of participation The Taking Part Survey, commissioned by the Department of Culture Media and Sport, placed Sunderland in the bottom 20% of local authority areas for arts

What Makes Sunderland A 'City Of Culture'?

engagement in the England. Only 37% of adults surveyed reported going to three or more mainstream cultural events a year, compared to 68% in Kensington and Chelsea.

It could be argued that this poses an interesting paradox in the heart of Sunderland's bid. In a city of low cultural engagement, would there be the community leadership or the support needed to make successful UK City of Culture bid? Yet whilst the findings of the Taking Part survey suggest one story, the reality of cultural engagement in the city in my experience is much more complex and nuanced.

In 2012 Arts Council England launched a programme called Creative People and Places, a programme only open to those areas of the country in the bottom 20% of participation according to the Taking Part survey and designed to explore and develop new ways to increase cultural engagement. In 2013 Arts Council England invested £2million into a three-year programme in Sunderland and South Tyneside called The Cultural Spring. Led by the University of Sunderland, the MAC Trust and the Customs House, the programme

focussed its attention in five wards in the north of Sunderland - Castle, Red House, Southwick, Fulwell and St Peters - and five neighbouring wards in South Tyneside.

It was working on Cultural Spring that brought me to Sunderland and it is the experience and learning from that project that has informed and shaped do much of my approach to the City of Culture bid.

The Cultural Spring sprang into action in April 2014 with a partnership with the BBC called the Great North Passion, a live retelling of the Easter Passion story broadcast to 1.3 million people from Bents Park in South Tyneside. It was a project that exemplified the Cultural Spring's ethos and ambition. Community art on a national platform, the Great North Passion was bold, ambitious, inclusive and democratic. It was a cultural melting pot that sought to express all art forms, all genres and all voices equally; from professional artists to those who would not define themselves as artists at all.

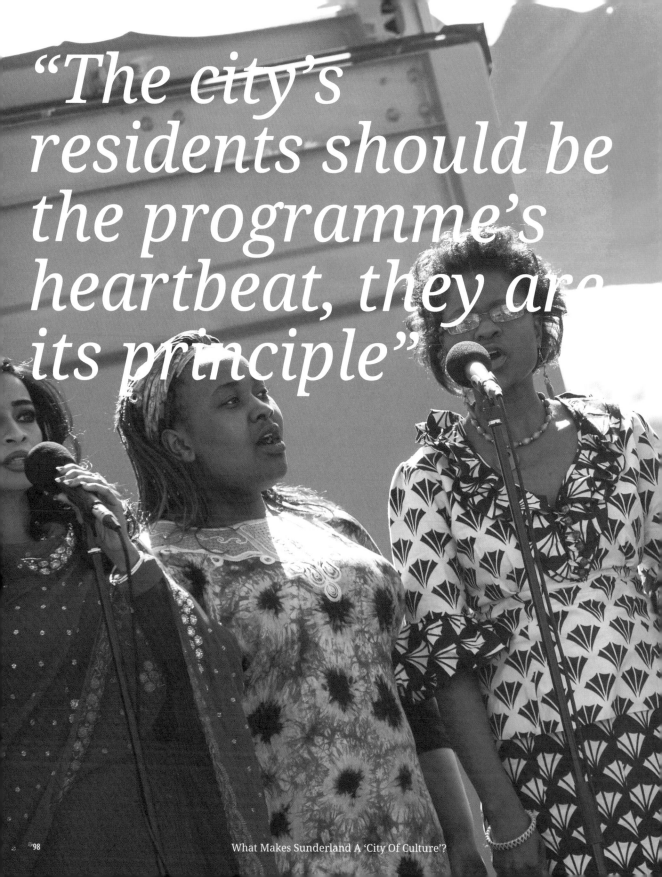

"The city's residents should be the programme's heartbeat, they are its principle"

What Makes Sunderland A 'City Of Culture'?

Rebecca Ball

What Makes Sunderland A 'City Of Culture'?

THE GREAT NORTH PASSION

The Great North Passion was the launch event for the Cultural Spring, the Arts Council England supported Creative People and Places project in Sunderland and South Tyneside. It was the BBC's flagship Easter programme and was televised live on BBC 1 on Good Friday, 2014 and was watched throughout the UK and abroad. In front of a live audience in Bents Park, South Shields, a series of live performances and art installations explored twelve universal themes.

The Great North Passion consisted of twelve shipping containers, that had been placed across the North East in the run up to the televised event. Each shipping container had an associated artist whose task it was to work with the local community to create an artwork representing one of the Stations of the Cross. These shipping containers were then transported to Bents Park where, along with almost forty others, they were combined to form an arena in the shape of a cross.

The event itself saw the large audience enjoy performances from X-Factor winner Alexandra Burke, Ross Millard and Jaff Craig of Futureheads fame, and opera singer Graeme Danby. Hosted by Fern Britton, and watched by a television audience of millions, The Great North Passion marked a hugely successful landmark beginning to the Cultural Spring's work in Sunderland and South Tyneside.

The Great North Passion won Best Event Tyneside and Best Overall Event at the 2014 Journal North East Culture Awards. At its peak, 1.3m viewers watched the broadcast. Viewing figures claimed more than a third of North Easterners watching TV at that time were watching the broadcast. The project was the culmination of six week's worth of community engagement. It brought together more than 20 artists with 12 local communities including schools, churches, community associations and heritage sites to explore different themes of Christ's Passion - Truth, Burden, Exhaustion, Loss, Kindness, Falling, Hope, Humility, Forgiveness and Self Sacrifice. Twelve red shipping containers, each representing an individual theme or Station of the Cross, were transformed with a variety of different interpretive art forms and placed in the park, forming the shape of a massive cross. More than 3,500 people attended the event and subsequent weekend exhibition. Shipping container content included bespoke pieces of music, intricate lighting displays, sculptures, spray paint murals, poetry and photography projects. It was a magnificent start to Sunderland and South Tyneside's 'Cultural Spring'.

CULTURAL SPRING COMMUNITY WORKSHOP PROGRAMME

Since 2014 the Cultural Spring has been engaged in creating a series of high quality cultural and artistic events across Sunderland and South Tyneside. Alongside these major events, the Cultural Spring has also been responsible for delivering an extensive and varied workshop programme, offering local residents opportunities to engage with new art forms, learn new skills and meet new people. From the very beginning these seasonal workshop programmes have embodied Cultural Spring's mission to engage more people and local communities in arts and culture.

Activity workshops include photography, jewellery making, song writing, ceramics, glass fusing, local storytelling, learning to play the ukulele, creative writing, digital imaging, sewing and textiles, drama, singing groups and much more and the workshop programme is designed to offer something new for everybody to try.

Working closely with the local communities, the Cultural Spring team has ensured the workshops delivered what local people were interested in, and over the last three years the programmes have been refined and honed with the help and experience of workshop attendees. Venues are carefully chosen to ensure the workshops were delivered in places as close as possible to residents' homes and have included coffee shops, churches, community centres and workingmen's clubs. They provide opportunities for people to come along and learn a new skill or art form, and to socialise and form new relationships with people who share similar interests.

Since it was launched the workshop programme has taken on something of a life of its own, spawning a number of standalone groups that have taken their developing skills and displayed them at public performances. Examples include the Hylton Ukes who now meet twice a week and came

together through ukulele workshops held in the Hylton Castle ward. Hylton Ukes have performed live at events including A Great Night Out, Summer Streets and Mr. Drayton's Human Jukebox.

Working with existing groups, and with other cultural activities and events across Sunderland and South Tyneside, the Cultural Spring's workshop programme has also produced work as part of the 14-18 Now Asunder project exploring the legacy of the Battle of the Somme.

The Cultural Spring's workshops have also provided residents with opportunities to work on some amazing projects from huge dance performances featuring hundreds of participants, to creating artwork for exhibition and meeting influential artists. RUSH and Wordplay workshops gave residents the opportunity to be taught by professional dance group Southpaw and take part in large-scale, choreographed productions.

Working closely with schools, Ship of Light workshops allowed people to design their own bottles and have them featured in the display as part of the 2016 Sunderland Illuminations.

Lindsay Kemp, the man who taught Kate Bush and Bowie to dance, led workshops giving local people the chance to interact and learn from a hugely respected artist.

The workshop programmes encourage inclusivity, break down barriers and create new and varied ways to engage, helping us achieve our ultimate aim of leaving a lasting legacy of communities with a genuine and abiding interest in arts and culture.

What Makes Sunderland A 'City Of Culture'?

"Alf exemplifies that DIY spirit so fundamental to Sunderland's character - if it's not here let's just make it happen!"

From Great North Passion, the Cultural Spring continued along this eclectic yet inclusive cultural vein. Working with local partners we commissioned and supported community proggy-mat sessions, school workshops with national ballet companies, miniature street art portraits, drop in opera roadshows. We wanted to be a catalyst for the broadest range of artistic activity in the area – certain that if we did – all of the 100,000 residents would find something they loved.

We didn't reach everybody but a magnificent amount of people did get involved. By the end of the second year the Cultural Spring had worked with well over 20,000 people. Not bad for an area of supposedly low cultural engagement. What was most remarkable, however, was not only the participation figures but also the leadership, passion and drive shown by so many of the people who got involved. Time and time again we met people with a certainty about what they wanted to get involved in, a willingness to take risks, a determination to shape the local cultural offer and a belief that the arts would have a positive impact on where they lived.

Alf and the Hylton Ukes

So I wanted to highlight a few examples of the remarkable community members who I've had the privilege to meet through their involvement in the Cultural Spring over the past few years and who for me epitomise that spirit of Sunderland's City of Culture bid. From Hylton Castle, Alf is the founder and leader of the Hylton Ukes. In his mid 70s Alf came along to a Cultural Spring community meeting and talked about his love for the ukulele and how he wanted to be able to play with a local group 'on his doorstep'. From this meeting (and with only the tiniest ounce of encouragement from Cultural Spring) he took it upon himself to set up a weekly Uke session. Little did we know that Alf had hit on the zeitgeist and his small weekly workshops rapidly grew to 30 people meeting twice a week to play ukulele classics together in the workmen's club in Hylton Castle. Before long they were touring local community groups and performing at events across the city. Taking on starring roles in large-scale commissions by Wildworks and Steve Drayton. Alf exemplifies that DIY spirit so fundamental to Sunderland's character – if it is not here let's just make it happen!

John and St Andrews Church Choir

From Roker, John first got involved with the Cultural Spring through the Great North Passion when the St Andrews Choir sang a new commission by Will Todd in a project led by operatic bass Graeme Danby. John volunteered to take part in a number of our commissioning panels. A retired vet John's constant refrain was "Well of course I am no expert" Or "I don't really know anything about this" but contrary to his assertions John's instinct for what would work and what wouldn't was fantastic. It is thanks to John that we commissioned Putting the Band Back Together, Wildworks and Mr Draytons Human Jukebox. What drove John's instinct for a great project? I think it was an openness, warmth and affability - all characteristics prevalent in a city that prides itself on its friendliness.

Sandra and the RUSHETTES

From Washington, Sandra responded to an advert the Cultural Spring put out encouraging adults with little or no previous dance experience to come along and get involved in a community dance project called RUSH. A brave act in itself! Sandra then performed along with 100 over people in an amazing show in front of St Hilda's Pit Head in South Shields. A couple of weeks later I saw Sandra and she said that the group of women she rehearsed with 'the RUSHETTES' had decided to keep meeting and had booked the hall to keep dancing. Again that DIY spirit! I then saw Sandra at a community opera roadshow – run by Sunderland's Music in the Minster. 'I have never sung before' she laughed. six months later she was performing on stage at the Sunderland Minster in the chorus of a new libretto 'Miracle' written by David Almond. The next time I saw Sandra she was taking part invigilating the exhibition of the group she'd got involved with at Grace House in Southwick and then shortly after she took up photography. A joy in discovering new things and openness to take risks – Sandra is a real cultural pioneer.

RUSH

What Makes Sunderland A 'City Of Culture'?

A six-month project looking at mass action and how arts and culture can provide an alternative to violent protest, RUSH was a Cultural Spring commission delivered in the spring of 2015. Featuring 150 dancers brought together over months of rehearsals, RUSH sought to explore the power of dance, music and writing to provide a voice to those disengaged or disenfranchised from society.

Featuring mass movement dancing, free running, a water cannon and an armada of prams, RUSH was produced by Southpaw Dance Company and performed against the background of the Engine House at St Hilda's Colliery, South Shields, in April 2015. Following the stories of three people, a homeless man, a worker on a zero-hours contract and a young single mother, RUSH offered people from the community the opportunity to work with internationally acclaimed artists and dancers.

More than 500 people watched dancers from Sunderland, South Tyneside and County Durham perform a series of high-tempo set pieces in a forty minute spectacular on Easter Sunday, 2015.

BRING THE HAPPY

What Makes Sunderland A 'City Of Culture'?

An arts project mapping happiness across Sunderland and South Tyneside, Invisible Flock's Bring the Happy was commissioned in winter 2014.

The project aimed to spread some happiness on the streets, working in collaboration with production company, Invisible Flock, who had previously run the project across Europe and further afield, asking people to place their happy memories on giant maps of the cities and towns they live in.

A number of installations were created in Sunderland and South Tyneside, with local residents "donating" happy memories to the project over a five-week period. These memories were then recorded onto a "happiness map", forming part of an overall project about happiness across the world. This process saw more than 1,000 memories contributed by local people.

What emerged from the project weren't just personal happy memories, but a glimpse into the stories that make a place. Memories included first loves, regrets, births, weddings, chance encounters and life changing moments. The project culminated in three live shows hosted at the University of Sunderland's North Shore in late February. The musical performance re-told the collected stories from hilarious to heart breaking, uplifting to upsetting and was greeted by a rapturous reception from three packed houses.

Rebecca Ball

MR DRAYTON'S HUMAN JUKEBOX

Commissioned by the Cultural Spring, and working across Sunderland and South Tyneside for six months in 2014 and 2015, Mr Drayton's Human Jukebox captured people's most memorable songs, as well as the stories behind those choices. Comedian and BBC Radio Newcastle producer, Steve Drayton, collected hundreds of stories from across the Cultural Spring's ten target wards in Sunderland and South Tyneside, capturing stories both funny and moving.

Four events were held at the Smugglers pub in Roker, and Whitburn and Marsden Social Club, building towards a final event at Hylton Castle Workingmen's Club in Sunderland on January 30, 2015. Storytellers that evening included BBC Newcastle's Alfie Joey and Horrible Histories author, Terry Deary, but amongst the eleven people who spoke the majority were normal people from Sunderland and South Tyneside who had embraced the opportunity to be part of the project.

Mr Drayton's Human Jukebox formed the Winter Tales part of the Cultural Spring's programme for 2014-15.

Rebecca Ball

What Makes Sunderland A 'City Of Culture'?

STREET ART HEROES

Another major commission from The Cultural Spring, Street Art Heroes saw some of the world's leading street artists come to Sunderland to take part in a project shining a light on a unique art form. Artists from Morocco, Brazil, Canada, Australia and across the United Kingdom worked with local communities to unearth, identify and portray local heroes through portraits on pavements, sculptures and large street murals.

Famous street artists including Roadsworth, Ben Wilson, Alex Senna, L7M, Cityzen Kane, Bruce Mahalski, Toothfish, Eyez, Artista, Frank Styles and Will Alexander contributed work that was presented in public spaces across Sunderland and South Tyneside in the autumn of 2014. From tiny works like Ben Wilson's painting on discarded chewing gum to huge murals like Frank Styles and Eyez' fishtank mural in Fulwell, Street Art Heroes showcased a whole host of different styles and forms of street art, bringing the Cultural Spring's offer out onto the streets of Sunderland and South Tyneside.

What Makes Sunderland A 'City Of Culture'?

INVENTORS!

Inventors! saw Sunderland-born artist, designer, author and inventor, Dominic Wilcox work with 500 children and young people from across Sunderland and South Tyneside to produce a whole host of fascinating and ground-breaking inventions. A Cultural Spring project, Inventors! took Dominic into schools and other venues across Sunderland and South Tyneside during October and November 2015, during which more than 600 drawings of inventions were submitted, with a selection of those drawings chosen for subsequent production.

A group of children and young people with some of the most interesting designs worked with a series of artists, designers, manufacturers and glassmakers to turn their ideas into working prototypes. Inventions included an umbrella for ladybirds, a "splat baby holder" a self-watering pot, a "shouty camera", reverse binoculars and a high-five machine. The inventions were displayed in a pop-up exhibition space on Sunderland's Fawcett Street beginning in January 2016.

Inventors! became a viral hit on social media, and created huge interest from across the world including featuring in a documentary on the Discovery Channel in the United States. The project culminated in an Inventors! STEAM Co Day held at Monkwearmouth Academy on January 29, 2016. Speakers at the day included Sir Peter Bazalgette, Chairman of Arts Council England and Newcastle MP Chi Onwurah.

Leila and Year 7 Monkwearmouth Academy

Leila is definitely continuing Sunderland's proud heritage of invention, innovation and creativity. A pupil in Year 7 at Monkwearmouth Academy Leila took part in a workshop as part of the Inventors with Dominic Wilcox project which asked 600 people across the city to design new inventions and then a selection were chosen to be brought to life by local engineers, artists and makers. Leila designed the shady lamp that was then beautifully realised at the FabLab.

They are a few examples of the many remarkable people for school kids to retirees whose enthusiasm for getting involved in arts and culture in their spare time is shaping Sunderland's City of Culture Bid. I could have written about Sarah Louise, Lauren, Val, Eileen, Issac, Kenny Ram, Sophie Lisa Beresford and countless others.

And then of course there are the many artists in the city. Iain Rowen, Ross Millard and Marie Nixon who started the city's artists forum What Next Group, Padma Rao from Sangini (Hindi for friendship), Pop Recs DIY spirit.

Our challenge over the next years will be to engage everyone across the city so they can promote their talents and make the things they want to see happen in the city a reality.

As a city, Sunderland is defined by its people but how do we define the word 'culture'. A word that has a very contentious etymology and as Raymond Williams says.

"Culture is one of the two or three most complicated words in the English language. This is so partly because of its intricate historical development, in several European languages, but mainly because it has now come to be used for important concepts in several distinct intellectual disciplines and in several distinct and incompatible systems of thought"

Culture can sometimes be associated with an a elitist or an "intellectual snobbery". Yet it can also be used to talk about collective customs and achievements of a people. In terms of what culture means in Sunderland's City of Culture bid it needs to reflect the spirit of the people.It will be defined by an openness to ideas, a desire to make things happen, a belief in the importance of the imagination, and the power of cultural democracy

Diwali Mela

Mela means 'to meet' and thousands of people from across the region flock to Sunderland's Museum and Winter Gardens to meet friends and family, to celebrate and to engage in cultural activity celebrating the festival of light at the city's Diwali Mela. This festival acts as a catalyst to achieve community cohesion through arts, culture and heritage where ethnic and cultural communities from across the spectrum come together celebrate their cultures, drawing in audiences who have low engagement in the arts that many other cultural providers find 'hard to reach'.

Culture is in our DNA and it is the glue that binds communities together as people with diverse backgrounds meet, make friends, eat together, sing along and share stories. The Mela is a wonderful family event that showcases the fantastic diversity of Asian arts and culture and allowed people from all backgrounds to come together, get involved and discover the delights and challenges of our shared cultural identity within Sunderland.

With dance, craft, fashion, food stalls, bazaars and street performance reflecting the rich and complex variety of contemporary lives, the event has high quality creative programming and shared learning with more than 75% of attendees coming from non-Asian communities.

"Wow had a fabulous time at the Diwali festival. Fantastic watching all of the children and families learning about this beautiful culture

and taking part in the Bhangra dancing. My daughter loved the music and drums.

"A fantastic idea to both celebrate culture and bring everyone together. My daughter came with her best friend (whose family are Indian) and loved having a chance to share in her culture."

"A great taste of Indian culture. Music dancing food all fabulous. Thank you for bringing this to our city and the people of Sunderland.

Kam Chera

Creating a Cultural Quarter

WORDS BY *Hannah Matterson & Paul Callaghan*
Sunderland Music, Arts & Culture Trust

Creating a Cultural Quarter

"creating vibrant and bohemian communities driven by the artists"

Cosmopolitan cities have always been home to artists and cultural producers, with talented and creative people clustering in particular areas, these clusters evolving naturally by virtue of the particular geographical and economic peculiarities of the city in question. Examples of such naturally occurring cultural clusters include Soho in London, New York's Greenwich Village or the Left Bank in Paris. These are places in which favourable economic conditions, particularly low property prices, enabled artists to work and live within their means, creating vibrant and bohemian communities driven by the artists at their heart. This in turn led to these areas becoming fashionable and desirable destinations, increasing land values and resulting in the gentrification of previously depressed sections of the cities.

In recent decades a whole host of civic authorities, both within the United Kingdom and around the world, have sought to artificially engineer such cultural quarters. These developments follow the implicit rationale that by attracting cultural producers, and often by the creation of new cultural venues, an area of the city which has been regarded in the past as unattractive by businesses and residents will suddenly become exciting and desirable as a place to live and work. This will then lead to the regeneration of the area, increasing land values and boosting the local economy by creating a plethora of new culturally focused jobs.

The cultural quarter is sometimes seen by public authorities as an all-purpose solution to a whole host of pervasive social and economic woes. Yet in many cases the implementation of cultural quarter planning is ill-advised, ill-considered, or simply badly executed and it is only through an awareness of these failures that a planned cultural quarter scheme, such as that in Sunderland, can become a success.

Culture-led regeneration schemes, defined as a model in which "cultural activity is seen as the catalyst and

engine of regeneration", focus on a number of common goals. The vocabulary employed in each application can be different, but the goals can be roughly grouped into three categories:

• production;
• consumption; and
• regeneration.

Production goals relate to the levels of cultural production within an area, seeking to boost the local economy by creating sustainable jobs in cultural production, developing original cultural output that can then be exported across the country and the world.

Consumption goals focus on increasing cultural consumption, increasing audiences and creating the designated 'quarter' as an attractive destination for cultural visitors to the city. This also feeds into the wider economy of the area, often stimulating the night-time economy in particular, generating a non-cultural economic benefit as a by-product of the increasing cultural consumption.

Regeneration goals specifically relate to the built environment, and revolve around the maintenance, creation and renovation of buildings and other cityscape elements. In many cases, cultural quarters are anchored by the

development of 'flagship' buildings, which both represent a new element in a city's environment and act as a symbol of the development itself.

Each cultural quarter project is different, each seeking to meet economic, social and cultural targets in its own way, and according distinct priorities to each of the individual targets. Comparing a number of different cultural quarter projects, we can see the way in which the different targets have been prioritised, and the extent to which they have been achieved and by assessing the contrasting approaches adopted we can construct a vision and a strategy that produces an outcome that maximises the benefits of the project for the community and the city.

From the late 1980s, the relationships between cultural industry and cultural policy was forced to be changed through the recognition of uneven cultural development between the North and South of the UK and it was around this time that local and regional policy makers acknowledged culture as a way to improve economic development. Although London is seen as the largest creative cluster in the UK, it was Sheffield that helped promote local cultural industry policies, especially this notion of 'cultural quarters'. Sheffield has always seen itself as a city of makers and doers and over the last thirty years has grown into one of the largest creative

"A groundbreaking local government initiative that sought to stimulate the economy of a previously derelict zone in a city."

communities in the country. Much of this community is concentrated in Sheffield's Cultural Industries Quarter (CIQ), just between Sheffield Station and the city centre, an area that was once the home of cutlery workers and toolmakers. Sixteen listed buildings are within this triangle and historic workplaces sit next to 21st century creative enterprises. In 1981 Sheffield created its own Department for Employment and Economic Development (DEED) which aimed to "develop local cultural and media industries". Unfortunately, as this was one of the first initiatives of its kind, DEED lacked the knowledge and money to attract big businesses to the city and had an on-going battle for funds with central government. The late 1990s saw renewed support for local cultural initiatives and regional policies continued to recognise culture as an important factor for development. In the 2000s, Sheffield's creative quarter grew with the help of EU and central government funding, but by 2010 the recession had hit and initiatives for developing creative businesses stopped. Today Sheffield has highlighted the creative industries as one of four main areas of focus for funding, with the city's Cultural Industries Quarter employing over 3000 people.

Sheffield is a prime example of a cultural quarter project that placed a significant emphasis on one of the three goals, creative and cultural production, arguably to the detriment of the other goals and the project as a whole. It is a fascinating example, a groundbreaking local government initiative that sought to stimulate the economy of a previously derelict zone in a city economy transitioning away from heavy industry as

an economic base. In line with the political climate within Sheffield at the time, the Cultural Industries Quarter was the product of significant local authority intervention. The emphasis was on job creation in cultural production. This was partly because unemployment was the major issue, and partly because public funding from European national and local sources was available specifically for this purpose. Little attention was paid to consumption, in the form of café culture, retail outlets for cultural goods, or even cultural institutions open to the public. Although there were perfectly understandable reasons for focusing on production, not least the lack of disposable income across the population of Sheffield at the time, it has undoubtedly affected the way in which the Cultural Industries Quarter has evolved over the thirty years since its establishment in 1981. As it was initially established almost exclusively to create cultural and creative jobs, it has become difficult for the Quarter to alter its tone and purpose in later years. Despite its notion of being mixed use there has been a lack of retail and residential businesses in the area which has severely reduced street level activity and animation. Although the Sheffield CIQ must be regarded as a success on a number of levels, and its pioneering position amongst British cultural quarter projects recognised, it has notable shortcomings because of a lack of balance within the development itself. In particular, it has failed to generate the kind of positive and vibrant atmosphere which is necessary for a cultural quarter project to be regarded as an unqualified success; to emphasise production facilities alone is to ignore this crucial element of any 'buzz'.

Hannah Matterson & Paul Callaghan

There are examples of cultural quarters that have been led by the private sector and are commercially driven but there are few that are third sector initiatives. In most instances it is a single local authority.

NewcastleGateshead is a successful partnership of local authorities, joining up two distinct areas to build their cultural economy in order for both sides of the River Tyne to grow. The NewcastleGateshead initiative (NGI) was set up in 2000 and has done much to make Tyneside a cultural and creative hub. Its bid to be European Capital of Culture 2008 was a reflection of this and although it was unsuccessful the process of cultural regeneration continued with the attraction of large public cultural events and encouragement of local participation with the arts. Investment into new infrastructure has included The Baltic art gallery, the Sage music venue and Live Theatre's LiveWorks development. Partnerships between regional development bodies, both local authorities, Arts Council England and NGI has maintained strong focus on culture and allowed an understanding of

the needs and possible impacts of attracting creative sector businesses and practitioners to the region. This has also led to an increase in tourism which now employs over 10% of the region's population. These cultural policies have undoubtedly helped to improve both the image and the economy of the city-region.

While it is widely hailed as a huge success, the regeneration of the Quayside area, particularly in Gateshead, presents a perfect example of a project in which, up until now, the provision of cultural venues has been prioritised over the production of cultural output. The redevelopment of the Quayside, specifically since the construction of the Gateshead Millennium Bridge connecting the two has seen a marked boost to the area's night-time and non-cultural economy. This has seen the Quayside become one of the most important attractions for visitors to NewcastleGateshead, incorporating iconic new buildings and vibrant, exciting nightlife.

NewcastleGateshead Quayside is a good example of the successful pursuit of regeneration through active

intervention. Prior to the Quayside redevelopment, the area was severely depressed, lacking attractions for visitors and suffering economically as a result. The Baltic Flour Mills, now repurposed as BALTIC Centre for Contemporary Art had closed in 1982, at the loss of 170 jobs in the local economy. Despite remaining a notable local landmark, by the 1990s it had come to represent the failures of the local economy. The redevelopment of the building saw it celebrated as a symbol of a town and an area 'on the up', an identification which became a distinct advantage for the Quayside redevelopment as local people took 'ownership' as a source of local pride that regenerated a local identity as much as it did the local economy.

Alongside the redevelopment of the existing urban landscape, the Quayside redevelopment also saw the construction of entirely new flagship buildings, most notably Sage Gateshead, opened in 2004. Sage Gateshead occupies a commanding position on the south side of the Tyne, occupying a plot of previously derelict industrial

waste ground. This demonstrates the other side of the successful regeneration of the Quayside, the development of iconic new buildings which have been embraced by the local community, and now represent the place and the area to the region and the world. The active intervention and pursuit of regeneration through the redevelopment of the Quayside has revitalised a previously distressed area of both Newcastle and Gateshead and brought substantial economic benefit both. The redevelopment of the NewcastleGateshead Quayside demonstrates the way in which 'flagship' developments can be blended with existing, iconic sites, in order to create a vibrant and exciting environment for cultural activity.

The Warwick Commission Report Enriching Britain: Culture, Creativity and Growth highlights the generation of a sense of identity, place and community as one of the key functions of culture and cultural activity, transcending the economic benefits of a flourishing artistic and creative sector.

"The Quayside regeneration took advantage of positive identification with iconic buildings like the Baltic to ensure success of the cultural quarter project"

Certain cultural quarter projects choose to prioritise different goals, one prime example being that of the regeneration of NewcastleGateshead Quayside, in particular in the construction and redevelopment of facilities like the Sage and the BALTIC Centre for Contemporary Art.

Birmingham on the other hand have, although began in a similar situation to Newcastle-Gateshead, approached cultural policy making with the view of growing enterprises and focusing on the economic value of creativity. From the 1970s there was a manufacturing decline in the city so, in a bid to change the city's fortunes, Birmingham City Council adopted an ambitious economic regeneration policy aiming to develop cultural quarters and build on their knowledge economy. From the 1990s they developed the area of the city known as Eastside into a creative hub, enticing businesses dealing in multimedia, visual arts, music and graphic design to locate there following investment from both the public and private sector. This gave the area a positive identity that transformed it and created thousands of jobs.

When it began the process Birmingham City Council had no set plans about how to develop the city culturally, but by strategic thinking and using low cost work spaces, creative businesses have been able to grow in close proximity to each other. The way they have developed in particular places would suggest that there was already a "creative class" of people living in the city so they just needed some funding in order to begin to exploit their knowledge and creativity more. The Jewellery Quarter of Birmingham is Europe's largest exporter of Jewellery and here the city built on an already diverse area and has helped make the Birmingham's first Creative Village in 2010.

The Sunderland MACQ project will learn from other cities' experiences in creating a cultural quarter, seeking to incorporate iconic Sunderland landmarks like the Fire Station and the Empire into a cohesive and forward-looking area of the city, one with which Sunderland's population identifies and connects, one which they consider to be, in a meaningful way, 'theirs' while striking a balance between

Creating a Cultural Quarter

each of the common culture-led regeneration goals.

The creation of the Music, Arts and Culture Quarter in the centre of the city involves a major regeneration of the Edwardian heart of the city and focuses on a number of buildings or sites that are all within the Bishopwearmouth Conservation Area. As a defined geographic area, it incorporates a number of existing buildings including the Empire, the Fire Station and others as well as some development sites. Sitting next to Sunderland Minster, it is adjacent to the University and to both the Retail and Business Quarters. The MACQ project involves the redevelopment of historic buildings (the 1907 Fire Station, the 1901 Dun Cow and Londonderry pubs and the 1907 Magistrates Court), conversion of an existing modern building (the vacant Police Station) and the construction of some new build elements as part of a masterplan for the area. The buildings will be used for arts, creative and culture purposes and, when completed in 2019, the MACQ will include theatre, music and dance spaces, galleries, facilities

"The creation of the Music, Arts and Culture Quarter in the centre of the city involves a major regeneration of the Edwardian heart of the city"

Creating a Cultural Quarter

"...The MACQ project enhances current facilities and offers fresh and vibrant new opportunities for cultural engagement to residents and visitors."

for new cultural enterprises and music and artistic education centres and collectively will form the vibrant and creative cultural heart of the city.

The funding for this ambitious regeneration of the centre of Sunderland through arts and culture has come from a number of sources. The Heritage Lottery Fund was the first major funder to commit and this was followed by support both in cash and kind by Sunderland City Council, which has since become an enthusiastic and committed partner in the project. Arts Council England has committed capital funding for the Fire Station Auditorium with the remainder coming from the City Council and the MAC Trust and there has also been significant private sector investment in the MACQ project. This historic Edwardian area of Sunderland city centre already boasts one of the city's two most prominent cultural assets, the Empire Theatre, and the MACQ project enhances current facilities and offers fresh and vibrant new opportunities for cultural engagement to residents and visitors.

In addition, the redevelopment of the former Police Station into a Cultural and Creative Industries Centre will allow the MACQ to encourage the creation of new art and cultural content which is reflective of the unique traditions and values of Sunderland and the North East, by offering artists and creatives opportunities to work in a place that is both economically sustainable and creatively productive.

This will enable Sunderland's existing cultural businesses to base themselves in the heart of the city, whilst providing ample opportunities for the growth of new cultural enterprises.

Creating places where art and culture can be produced, practiced, delivered and enjoyed is at the very heart of the vision for the Sunderland MACQ. Sunderland's lack of small and medium sized cultural venues has been a direct obstacle to the cultural development of the city, and it is this problem that the Sunderland MACQ aims to solve. The redevelopment of the Fire Station and building the attached auditorium will add new cultural capacity to the city, with a range of facilities for dance, drama and music. It will enhance the city's existing flagship cultural venue at the Sunderland Empire, as well as complementing the burgeoning success of the newly renovated Dun Cow and the Peacock. The new facilities will work in concert with the existing venues to ensure that consumers regard Sunderland as a genuine cultural destination.

The development of the night time economy will both guarantee the financial viability of the associated cultural venues and allow visitors to eat, drink and engage in cultural activity all within the bounds of the MACQ. One of the most significant problems facing the area at the moment is the tendency for potential customers to 'drain away' following visits to the Sunderland Empire. The Empire sees over 300,000 visitors per year but there has been a poor offer attracting these visitors to remain within the area and spend their time and money. The MACQ's broader cultural offer, as well as the wider range of non-cultural consumption, will attract people to the cultural quarter on a more regular basis and keep them there for longer.

Sunderland has a relatively low participation rate in arts and culture and the MACQ development meets a latent need, providing an opportunity for new arts and theatre provision within the city to thrive.

Creating a Cultural Quarter

"Creating places where art and culture can be produced, practiced, delivered and enjoyed is at the very heart of the vision for the Sunderland MACQ."

Hannah Matterson & Paul Callaghan

THE AUDITORIUM

The MACQ will be both financially and environmentally sustainable, delivering new employment opportunities and economic benefits to the city, whilst using the revenue generated from the various restaurants and bars to subsidise and guarantee the delivery of high quality artistic content throughout the quarter and will form a new hub both culturally and economically, offering employment, training and volunteering opportunities to people from both Sunderland and the wider region.

This project started in 2013 and Phase One, completed in 2014, involved the renovation of the historic Dun Cow pub as a small-scale music venue and restaurant. One of the surviving jewels in the city's architectural crown, the Dun Cow was purchased, renovated and revitalised as both a pub and a cultural venue. Prior to this it was at a point where it was commercially unviable and structurally unsound. This beautiful Grade 2 listed building has been restored to its former glory and in 2016 won two prestigious national awards from Historic England, the Victorian Society and Camra. These were the National Restoration Award and the National Conservation Award and were recognition of the care and investment made into this magnificent building. It is now thriving commercially with a popular restaurant on the first floor and hosts a variety of music events and other cultural activities. It attracts a diverse clientele and has been highly praised for its painstaking restoration and attention to original detail.

The second phase has been the conversion of the Fire Station into a cultural hub. Originally built in 1907, it was operational until its closure in 1992. The building was bought by the MAC Trust and has undergone a major £3.6m redevelopment funded through grants from the Heritage Lottery Fund and Sunderland City Council and a significant investment from the MAC Trust. The building will house Dance City and drama and music studios operated by Live Theatre and a heritage centre celebrating the city's heritage with specific reference to its emergency services. A restaurant and cafe on the ground floor subsidises the cultural offer. The Londonderry, now The Peacock, is stage three in the MACQ programme. This magnificent 1901 building was once one of the city's finest but over recent years has become one of the city's most neglected buildings. It has now had a major redevelopment and refurbishment programme and its large first floor function room is again an arts and music venue with a capacity of 250 as it was in the 1960s and 70s when it played host to artists such as John Martyn, Bert Jansch and Sunderland-born Dave Stewart. It has been renamed The Peacock, the original name of the hostelry and coaching inn that stood on the site from 1770.

The fourth element in the project is the Fire Station Auditorium that will be built on a vacant site adjoining the Fire Station and next to the Empire. Sitting next to Sunderland Minster, it is adjacent to the University and to the Retail and Business Quarters. The multi-use auditorium is a major project that will use arts and culture as important catalysts for, and significant elements in, the regeneration of Sunderland. It involves a new build extension to the Fire Station incorporating a new multi-use auditorium providing theatre, music and performance space which will both act as the fulcrum for the quarter and complement the existing facilities within the surrounding area. The addition of the auditorium as an extension to the Fire Station, will allow for a significant diversification of the MACQ's cultural offer. The versatile space offered by the auditorium will allow it to become both a focal point for developing and showcasing Sunderland's indigenous artistic the arts and the education and cultural talent and also attract artists and performers both nationally and internationally. The advancement of of the public in the arts are core objectives of this project and the auditorium will be central to this advancement and education within both the city of Sunderland and the wider region as a whole. The auditorium's 450 seats will be retractable, allowing it to be converted into a 750-capacity standing venue for larger performances, significantly broadening Sunderland's cultural offer. Arts Council England has generously given a grant of £6 million towards the £8.2million cost of the building and it will open in July 2019.

The MACQ will encompass all of three elements discussed at the start of this chapter. It will be a place where art and cultural production can take place, where people of all ages and all backgrounds will learn to dance and act and sing and write music. It will act as magnet for artists from Sunderland and from elsewhere to come to produce and to stay. It will attract hundreds of thousands of people to come and see great art and community art, performances they know they will enjoy and new experiences that can change how they see the arts and culture and it will do all of this is an area, sitting at the heart of the city, that in its decline epitomised the downturn in Sunderland's fortunes over the last decades but which will now be regenerated and become a symbol of the city's hope for a successful future.

Asian Culture in Sunderland

One of the most influential artists of his generation, Gurdas Maan, the multi-awarding winning, artist, actor and songwriter, performed at the Sunderland Empire in 2017 celebrating Asian culture, traditions and diversity through his music.

It was the first time in 20 years that such a high-profile artist from India had performed in the region and the event brought together people of all ages from Indian and Pakistani backgrounds as well as non-Asians wanting to embrace the culture and atmosphere that this event created. It underlined Sunderland's growing reputation for its capacity to stage nationally and internally significant events.

Kam Chera

Sunderland's Cultural Heritage

WORDS BY *Rob Lawson*

Chair of Governors
Sunderland College

Sunderland's Cultural Heritage

"A celebration of Sunderland's maritime and industrial heritage. "

When work on Sunderland's new event space Keel Square was completed in 2015, much was made of how the square's Keel Line linked the city centre to the Wear. But the Keel Line is more than just a physical connection, it is an emotional and historical link to Wearside's proud heritage. A history that made Sunderland the city it is and its inhabitants the 'Mackems'.

At one end of the Keel Line is Stephen Broadbent's striking sculpture 'Propellers of the City', while its length echoes the largest ship ever launched on the Wear, the Naess Crusader launched from the James Laing shipyard in 1972. Along its 291m length, Sunderland artist Bryan Talbot has added the names of more than 8,100 vessels launched on the Wear over the centuries.

Keel Square was built as a public space, a place for events and activities – but it is also a celebration of Sunderland's maritime and industrial heritage and although shipbuilding and Wearside are synonymous, the industry was not the city's first. Nor was the city founded on the construction of ships.

Artefacts from Stone Age hunter-gatherers have been excavated from both St Peter's Church in Monkwearmouth and further west at Hastings Hill. It is thought the Celtic Brigante tribe occupied the Wearside area during the pre and post Roman era and although no direct evidence has been found, it is believed locally that there was a Roman settlement on what is now the former Vaux Brewery site on the southern bank of the Wear.

It is on the opposite bank of the river where we find the first recorded settlement on the Wear. Benedict Biscop, an Anglo-Saxon nobleman, was granted land by Ecgfrith, King of Northumbria from 670 until his death in 685. Biscop had earlier made pilgrimages to Rome, where he returned "full of fervour and enthusiasm … for the good of the English church," according to Victorian writer E.C.S. Gibson, author of Northumbrian Saints. With the land given to him, Biscop built a monastery in 674, bringing to Monkwearmouth masons from the Continent who could build in the pre-Romanesque style. Returning from his fifth and final trip to

Rome in 679, Biscop brought with him books and glaziers. Both were vital in the development of Sunderland.

The books formed the basis of a library that helped establish the twin Monkwearmouth-Jarrow monastery as one of the most important European centres of learning and education. It was a large library for its time, said to have consisted of 200 books, and manuscripts copied there became prized possessions and include the Codex Amiatinus, one of the earliest surviving manuscript of the Bible, now kept in Florence. Biscop, who was adopted as the Patron Saint of Sunderland in 2005, led the Monkwearmouth Monastery of St Peter's and it was here that a young seven-year-old boy named Bede first studied.

Young Bede became a monk and a scholar and is now known to the world as the Venerable Bede, or Saint Bede, and his most famous work, Historia Ecclesiastica Gentis Anglorum (The Ecclesiastical History of the English People) gained him the title 'The Father of English History'. The glaziers Biscop brought over from France and Rome made stained glass windows for the Monkwearmouth priory – but also introduced glass making to England on a site only

yards from the National Glass Centre, opened on the north bank of the Wear in 1998. The production of glass was to become a part of Sunderland's industrial heritage.

The importance of the Monkwearmouth-Jarrow monastery started to wane after the deaths of Biscop in 690 and Bede in 735 and in the wake of Viking raids on the north east coast in the latter part of the eighth century. The monastery was attacked in 794 and then again in about 860. It was finally abandoned in the late ninth century and was later dissolved by Henry VIII in 1545 when King granted its lands to Thomas Whitehead, of Durham. Part of this area is still today known as 'Monkwearmouth', referring back to the days of St Peter's monastery. In 930 Athelstan of England gave the Bishop of Durham lands south of the Wear and that area became known as 'Bishopwearmouth'.

By 1100 this parish included a fishing village known as 'Soender-land' – land cut asunder or put to one side. The name evolved into Sunderland, and in 1179 the town was granted a charter by Bishop of Durham Hugh Du Puiset (Pudsey) who at the same time granted charters for both Durham and Gateshead.

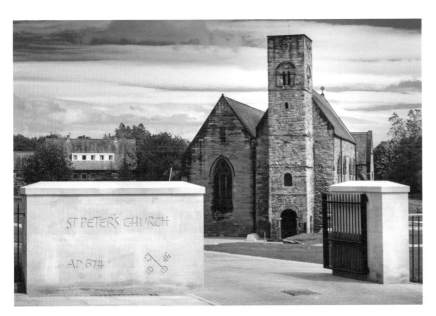

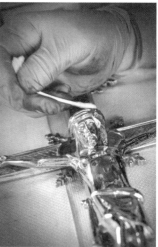

Sunderland city centre as we know it was originally Bishopwearmouth and was not part of the 'real' Sunderland that was further to the east, much closer to the mouth of the Wear. The area is now home to the Port of Sunderland and is known as the East End or Old Sunderland. It is populated with riverside apartments and offices, but in its prime was probably the busiest part of town

The three settlements of Monkwearmouth, Bishopwearmouth and Sunderland had separate identities, but were connected by ferries and streets. The connection from Sunderland to Bishopwearmouth was Wearmouth High Street. With its busy dockside, Sunderland was fast becoming the more prosperous of the three villages, and the main focus for growth on Wearside. In 1712, Sunderland merchants began a campaign for their own parish church, tired with the long walk to the church at Bishopwearmouth and eager to forge their own identity. Seven years later they got their wish, and Holy Trinity Church was consecrated on September 5, 1719 as the church of the newly created Parish of Sunderland. Although the area around it has changed massively in the 300

running from the Old Garrison and Barracks west through dense housing and quays along the river, continuing through more affluent housing and private gardens to Bishopwearmouth green two miles up river. Wearside's industries of coal, glassmaking and lime quarrying expanded, attracting more and more people looking for work on the river or on the docks. The port area became overcrowded, with folk packed into tenements, many of which were conversions of large homes whose owners had moved west.

By the 19th century, High Street was lined with markets selling all manner of goods and services. Low Street, packed with taverns, ran parallel. In 1814, the Exchange Buildings opened on High Street. The building was Wearside's first town hall, replacing the temporary base at Holy Trinity Church. It was paid for by public subscription, with £8,000 raised through shares sold at £50. Investors were rope makers, brewers and even portrait painters and Newcastle architect John Stokoe was drafted in to design the commercial, cultural and administrative centre. It incorporated a post office, a magistrates' court, kitchens and even a newspaper reading

"The church was at the heart of the bustling port, housed the city's first library and at one point was the base for the local fire engine."

years since it was built, Holy Trinity is instantly recognisable as when the first rector, Daniel Newcombe, took up his position. The church was at the heart of the bustling port, housed the city's first library and at one point was the base for the local fire engine. The clock face was added in 1856, but by this time the focus of commercial and civic activity had moved west and by the 20th century, Holy Trinity had almost been cut adrift from the city centre. It survived minor damage during German bombing raids in the early 1940s, but could not survive rising maintenance bills and dwindling congregations. The last regular service was held on June 26, 1988. The Grade 1 listed building is now in the care of the Churches Conservation Trust and is being restored with support from The Heritage Lottery Fund. The fund is working with the University of Sunderland, Sunderland City Council and Hendon Young People's Project on The Canny Space project that aims to transform the church into a centre for stories celebrating the area's rich history.

Detailed maps of the 18th century show High Street

room and played host to magnificent banquets and social events. The Duke of Wellington and later Sir Walter Scott, playwright and poet, attended dinners. The cholera epidemic of 1831 was the catalyst for a period of decline for the building, although it enjoyed some resurgence in fortunes and by 1914 was home to several companies and a bank. By the 1960s, however, it was standing empty once again. Thankfully, in 1996 the North of England Civic Trust, supported by the city council and English Heritage restored the building and it is now once again hosting dinners, banquets and parties. Adjacent to the Exchange Buildings is another city landmark, the former Eagle Tavern. Records for the site show a long history of inns, but the existing tavern was built in or around 1869. Previous taverns there included the Three Crowns, the Exchange Tavern and the Royal Exchange, but the Eagle Tavern took its name from a carved wooden eagle which gazed down from its pediment. It closed in 1920, becoming a Bakelite plastic factory. The building was restored in 2002, gaining a new eagle carved by sculptor Phil Townsend.

Rob Lawson

Overcrowding of the East End had reached dangerous levels when cholera struck in 1831 and spread rapidly. It was probably brought into the port on flax imported from Latvia, where cholera was rampant. The epidemic took hold among people living in quayside squalor and took four months to get under control. By then 215 people, including the hero of the Battle of Camperdown, Jack Crawford, had died. It took more than 20 years to understand the disease had spread through unsanitary water and a further 20 years before the local authority provided adequate drainage. Sunderland and Bishopwearmouth continued to move toward each other until they became one. Old Sunderland's packed housing remained a problem until modern council houses and flats replaced the old housing in the 1950s and 1960s. Now the only links are a few buildings and the old street names.

Bishop Pudsey, the same Prince Bishop who had granted the town a charter, also commissioned several ships to be built at Sunderland to carry troops to the crusades, but it was not until just over 160 years later in 1346 that merchant Thomas Menville was granted a charter allowing him to build ships on the Wear. From that year until December 7, 1988 when the last shipyard closed, Sunderland had more than 400 registered shipyards, becoming the largest shipbuilding town in the world and ships made in the city spread the name of Sunderland around the globe.

In the late the 16th century salt was being made in Sunderland. The process of salt panning saw seawater being heated by coal, evaporating the water and leaving salt. This new industry, based around Bishopwearmouth Panns, later know as Pann's Bank, gave further impetus to two growing industries. Coalmining was needed to hue the coal for the heating of the saltwater and shipbuilding to create the vessels needed to export the salt, as well as glass products from an expanding glass industry.

Inferior quality coal was used for salt panning, but a mining community started to evolve and better quality coal, found beneath the ground throughout the area began to be exported to London and East Anglia from the town's new port.

It was improvements to the port in the 18th century that allowed further expansion of shipbuilding in the town. The improvements meant larger ships could use the Wear to export salt, coal and glass.

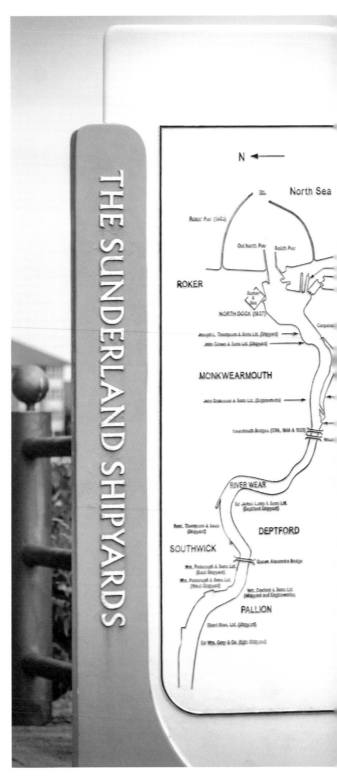

Sunderland's Cultural Heritage

After its initial introduction by Benedict Biscop in the 7th century, modern glassmaking on Wearside began in the 1690s when the first glasshouses opened in Deptford. Although ornamental glass and tableware was manufactured, most of the glass being produced at this time was for windows and bottles.

Sunderland's glassmaking industry reached its height during the middle of the 19th century when the new technique of 'pressing' made mass production possible. The industry was also helped by the ready supply of cheap coal and high-quality sand that could be brought in through the port.

Pyrex glassware was manufactured in Sunderland, but in 2007 the last two remaining glass firms in the city – Corning Glass Works and Arc International (who made Pyrex) announced they were to close.

By 1790 the town was producing 19 ships a year; in early 1814 31 ships were under construction at 23 yards and by 1815 about 600 ships were built in 31 yards. The town had become the biggest producer of wooden trading ships in the world.

The port flourished and further improvements were made to the port including Hudson North Dock opening in 1837, South Dock in 1850 and Hendon Dock in 1868. By 1840, the number of yards had increased to 76 and improved techniques had allowed the yards to build more and bigger ships. By the middle of the 19th century, production had increased from two to up to five vessels a week. During the period 1846-1854 almost one third of ships built in the UK were made in Sunderland, justifying the Sunderland Herald's claim that the town was "the greatest shipbuilding port in the world." Shipyards with international reputations opened including Austin and Son in 1826, William Pickersgill in 1851 and William Doxford in 1840.

As steam power replaced sail, and iron replaced wood, yards introduced engine works, adding to the skills and jobs needed on the Wear. In 1868, production of wooden vessels was, for the first time, surpassed by the creation of iron frame and wooden hull ships. The last wooden ship was built in 1880, just as steel replaced iron and the last sailing ship was built on the Wear in 1893. By the turn of the century, the Wear was mainly producing cargo ships and tankers, about a quarter of which were being produced for customers abroad.

As a result of the change from wooden to iron and then steel construction, the number of yards on the Wear decreased although tonnage rose. During the First World War, there were only 16 yards on the river and by the outbreak of the Second World War, the number had halved again, although a ninth yard was opened on the site of the former Swan, Hunter and Wigham Richardson yard during the war years. The role of the Wear during both world wars was to produce cargo ships to keep vital supply lines in and out of the country open. There was also plenty of naval construction and repair work to be done. The war years also led to another change and women were employed in the yards for the first time.

It is thought that the Wear yards were the origin of the word 'Mackems', by which Wearsiders are sometimes known. The history of the word is still debated, but most people believe it to relate to the phrase 'We Mack'em (make them) and they Tack'em (take them).' Wearsiders made the ships and Tynesiders fitted them out. The term has come to refer to someone from Sunderland, particularly supporters of Sunderland AFC. Although originally meant as an insult, many Wearsiders are now happy to be called a Mackem and for some it is worn as a badge of pride.

During the post-war years, Sunderland continued to be the country's pre-eminent shipbuilder, but competition was growing. As production increased globally and new nations entered the shipbuilding world, it became more and more difficult for Sunderland and other British yards to compete. Yards closed or merged across the country throughout the 1950s and 1960s and in 1977 the British shipbuilding industry was nationalised, leading to big job losses and many of them were on the Wear. In 1978 the yards employed 7535 people, six years later that number had reduced to 4337. The city's last two remaining shipyards merged, but it was too late and in December 1988, despite furious opposition locally, the last Wear yard closed.

Devastatingly for Sunderland, at the same time as the shipyards were closing, so were the town's other main source of employment – the mines.

With stunning coastal and riverside views, it is hardly surprising Sunderland has a tradition of inspiring artists. One such artist was Clarkson Frederick Stanfield (1793 – 1867) regarded as the greatest British marine artist of his day. Born in the city the son of an Irish actor and former seaman, Clarkson worked as a coach decorator until he stepped on board a South Shields collier to become a sailor. He joined the Royal Navy in 1808, serving until 1814 until he was discharged. A voyage to China followed, with Stanfield returning with a book full of sketches.

Soon after his return in 1816 Stanfield was employed by the Royalty Theatre in Wellclose Square, London, as a scene-painter and general decorator. His artistic talents were clear and in 1823 he moved to the more important Drury Lane Theatre as resident scene-painter. He stayed there until 1834, by which time his name and fame had spread. Stanfield

returned to theatre painting for two particular friends – designing scenery for Charles Dickens and William Charles Macready.

Working with partner David Roberts, Stanfield was an early pioneer of the 'moving panorama.' These were huge paintings that were turned into dramatic shows by adding sound and lighting.

Two of these panoramas – Venice and its Adjacent Islands and The Military Pass of the Simplon - were inspired by an 1830 tour to Italy and Germany. The scale of these works is impressive – the Venetian scene was more than 300 feet long and about 20 feet high.

During these years Stanfield was also developing his skills as a marine artist, first exhibiting at the Royal Academy in 1820. Four years later, he helped establish the Society of British Artists, becoming its President in 1829.

> "Three years after his death the Royal Academy hosted a major retrospective of his work."

From 1820 until his death in 1867, Stanfield contributed popular works to the Academy, the most famous of which were his marine paintings. The public loved the immediacy and drama of his paintings, preferring them to J.M.W. Turner's later maritime work. John Ruskin was a great admirer, lavishing praise on his attention to detail, his powerful skies and his ability to portray movement and the transparency of water.

His most impressive work is the huge Battle of Trafalgar, painted in 1836 and now hanging in the United Services Club in London. The work combines his knowledge of the sea, his expertise of drawing ships and his scene painter's ability for working on a large-scale piece. Another of his most well known work, the Castle of Ischia, is now in Sunderland Museum and Art Gallery. Other works at the Wearside venue include Chasse-Maree off the Gull Stream Light (1838) and The Dreadnought off Greenwich (1850-57).

Three years after his death the Royal Academy hosted a major retrospective of his work. The Times wrote: "There are no English painters whose works have won wider and warmer popularity outside the artistic pale. Stanfield's practiced command of the artist of composition, his unerring sense of the agreeable and picturesque in subject and effect, his pleasant and cheerful colour and last, not least, the large use to which he turned his knowledge and love of the sea and shipping… (all) added to the widespread admiration he had won by his consummately skilful scene painting, (and) combined to make him one of the most popular, if not the most popular, of landscape painters."

Other painters captured images of important vessels designed and built on the Wear. The Torrens, for instance, was a clipper ship designed to carry cargo and passengers between the UK and Australia. Built by James Laing and launched in 1875 she was the fastest ship to sail the London-Adelaide route and Joseph Conrad served as the ship's chief officer before beginning his career as a writer. Montague Dawson and Canadian artist Jack L Gray both immortalised the vessel on canvas, while the Winter Gardens has a large model of the ship on display.

Another famous Sunderland clipper, the City of Adelaide, has also been the subject of artists. Built by William Pile, Hay and Co for transporting passengers and cargo in 1864, and like the Torrens, she also held the record for passage from London to Adelaide. The vessel was later used for carrying coal and as a hospital ship. In 1923 she was commissioned in the Royal Navy as HMS Carrick. She reverted to her original name during a ceremony hosted by the Duke of Edinburgh in 2013.

Her importance as one of the last surviving emigrant ships led to a long battle for restoration. In late November 2013 she was loaded on to a cargo ship and arrived in Port Adelaide in February 2014 where restoration work is continuing.

The most prominent artist to paint City of Adelaide was Liverpudlian John Alcott who emigrated to Australia where he painted both Adelaide (1938) and the Cutty Sark. The nation's most popular 20th century painter, L.S. Lowry, also used Sunderland ships in his paintings. From 1960, Lowry used Room 104 at what is now the Marriott on the seafront as a base for working. Some of the many paintings he completed in the city include ships and boats on the Wear, while others portray the industry of the river. The area served both as an escape and an inspiration for the artist: "I like Sunderland because of the shipping, shipbuilding and countryside. I like the sea. I sometimes escape to Sunderland. I get away from art and artists."

His favourite spots included the River Wear, overlooking Lambton Drops, as well as the shipyards and the seafront. The Winter Gardens has the largest collection of Lowry's work outside of his birthplace in the North West.

Just as shipbuilding, the city's coal-mining heritage dates back centuries. There is evidence of coal being excavated in the north east by the Romans, but it wasn't until the 13th and 14th centuries that coal mining became more widespread in the region.

Newcastle's coal lay in shallow, accessible seams close to the Tyne, but Sunderland's coal was deep underground. Ready access to Tyneside's coal gave Newcastle a natural advantage and the city had a virtual monopoly on exporting coal, to the disadvantage of rival ports like Sunderland. However, as Tyneside's became exhausted Sunderland's deep reserves attracted serious prospecting. Earlier explorations had failed to find any significant measures in the Durham coastal limestone.

Little coal was found in Sunderland during more extensive excavations at Pallion in 1788, West Herrington in 1806 and Hylton Castle in 1816, although coalmines were opening in surrounding areas like Newbottle in 1774, Lumley in 1776, Washington F Pit in 1777 and Penshaw in 1791. In 1820 good quality coal was found under magnesium limestone in Hetton, seven miles west of Sunderland. Elemore, Houghton, Pittington and North Hetton collieries followed Hetton Colliery's 1822 lead.

Four years later, the sinking of Pemberton Main, what was to become Wearmouth Colliery, began. The coal stream was finally struck in October 1834, 1,578 feet below sea level and Wearmouth pit was then the deepest mine in the world. The wait to find the coal seam had been a huge strain on the resources of the mine's owners, Messrs Thompson, Pemberton and Co, but in the summer of 1835 the company loaded its first cargo of coal on to a Wear ship from staiths built by the colliery to transfer coal directly from the pit on wagons running on inclined gravity planes.

For 160 years, Wearmouth Colliery was one of Sunderland's biggest employers and owned large areas of the town. Its underground tunnels went miles out to sea in search of coal and in 1958 the colliery was earmarked as a super pit, with investment to exploit the 500 million tons of undersea coal. Improvements were made and by 1960, there were almost 40 miles of underground roadways. More than 2,000 men were employed at the pit and output reached 11,500 tons a week. Other substantial pits were established at Ryhope in 1859, Silksworth, also known as as New Tunstall in 1873 and Hylton, also known as Castletown, in 1900.

Rob Lawson

"A celebration of Sunderland's maritime and industrial heritage."

All of these had their own communities that spread from the pitheads and each employed hundreds of local men. By 1947, when the industry was nationalised, there were more than 130 collieries within the Durham Coalfield, employing more than 100,000 people.

Cheap oil, natural gas, nuclear power and cheap foreign imports began to take their toll and mines began to close in the early 1960s. In ten years, 70 mines closed and 60,000 men lost their jobs. Ryhope closed in 1966, Silksworth, which had only recently been modernised, followed in 1971 and then Hylton Colliery closed in 1979. The last shift at Wearmouth, which had become one of the largest and most important pits in the Durham Coalfield, left the pit on December 10, 1993, ending eight centuries of coal mining tradition in the region. Six hundred and seventy men lost their jobs, but the mine did not close without a fight. As they had in the 1984 Miners' Strike, MPs, unions and councillors fought to save the pit. Initially, it was thought a private mining firm would save Wearmouth, the UK's oldest pit. But, despite enormous reserves of coal still lying under the sea, nothing could save

Wearmouth. The site was cleared and a famous Sunderland landmark was set to be replaced by a new one.

As Sunderland ships and shipbuilding inspired art and artists, so did the city's other main industry. And most of those inspired by the mines also worked down them. Although Norman Cornish was born in nearby Spennymoor, his connections to the city were strong. Cornish began working in the mines in 1933 aged only 14. A year later he joined the famous Spennymoor Settlement's Pitman's Academy and started drawing and painting what he saw around him. He went on to become a celebrated and accomplished artist, and the last of the Pitmen Painters made famous by Lee Hall's popular play.

Cornish, who became friends with L.S. Lowry, left the mines in 1966 because of chronic back pain, and had to rely on his art to make a living. Thankfully, he was offered a visiting lectureship at what was then Sunderland College of Art, a position that allowed him to complete the transition from miner to artist. Cornish was awarded an Honorary Doctorate of Arts from the University of Sunderland in 2012,

and after his death in 2014, his family gifted his painting Pit Road to the University. It is now on permanent display in National Glass Centre's Stories of Glass exhibition – hanging alongside a sketch of St Peter's by L.S. Lowry.

SAFC's Stadium of Light is one of the UK's best stadia and a place of regular pilgrimage for thousands of supporters. The stadium was opened in July 1997 and now has a capacity of about 49,000 spectators. Its name was significant, as then SAFC Chairman Bob Murray explained: "The name was chosen for two reasons: as an ever-lasting tribute to the region's mine-workers and proud industrial heritage and in the expectation that the stadium would be a guiding light in the future. The name is very much a symbolic link to the thousands of miners and Sunderland supporters that emerged from the darkness and into the light every day when they returned to the surface after working in the mine." To emphasise the theme, a permanently lit, oversized Davy Lamp stands at the entrance to the stadium.

The modern stadium is a far cry from SAFC's first ground – the Blue House Field in Hendon where, in 1879, the Sunderland and District Teachers' Association Football Club first played. James Allan, a graduate of Glasgow University, who had started teaching at Hendon Board School, set up the club. Allan was later to leave the club and establish a rival club called Sunderland Albion. In 1882, 'The Lads' played in blue and employed a 2-2-6 formation.

Six years later, the 'Team of all the Talents' as Sunderland were dubbed, was elected to the fledgling Football League, with their first league game a 2-3 home defeat against Burnley. The club went on to win the league in 1892, 1893 and 1895 and moved into its new Roker Park home in 1898.

Over the years the club has enjoyed some memorable moments. In 1908, the club recorded what still remains as the top-flight's biggest away win – a 9-1 hammering of Newcastle United. In 1913, the club reached the FA Cup Final for the first time, losing to Aston Villa who they'd beaten to the league title. The 1930s brought great success – league champions in 1936 and FA Cup winners in 1937, with local hero and England international Raich Carter captaining the team.

After the Second World War, Len Shackleton, the Clown Prince of Soccer, entertained huge crowds with his exceptional talent. In the 1949-50 season, Sunderland's total gates were more than a million with an average of almost 48,000. The team missed winning the championship by one point, finishing third.

During the 1950s, Sunderland spent big, earning the nickname, 'The Bank of England' Club. The money didn't bring success, however. Despite finishing fourth in the league and enjoying an FA Cup semi-final appearance in 1955, the club was relegated for the first time in 1958. The legendary manager, Brian Clough, was part of the team rebuilt by manager Alan Brown in order to regain First Division status but Clough was injured in a game on Boxing Day 1962 and his playing career ended at the age of 28. Even without his prolific goal scoring, the club returned to the top flight in 1964, though a second relegation followed in 1970. New manager Bob Stokoe produced what is still remembered as the club's finest moment when Sunderland beat the mighty Leeds in the FA Cup final, the first time a second tier team had won the cup in 40 years.

The victory did not lead to sustained success as the club 'yo-yo-ed' from first to second division and back again. In 1987, Sunderland were relegated to the Third Division. They bounced straight back the following year and in 1990 were promoted to the First Division, having beaten Newcastle in a play-off semi-final. Relegation followed, but Peter Reid regained Premiership status in 1995, before once again dropping down a division.

Rob Lawson

The move from Roker Park to the Stadium of Light came in 1997, and in their first season in their new home, the club reached the play-off final against Charlton Athletic. It is a game still talked about by fans and neutrals, and which Sunderland lost 7-6 on penalties, having drawn 4-4 during normal time. With fans favourite Kevin Phillips in the side, the team powered back into the Premiership the following season, with a record-breaking 105 points and the third-highest attendance figures in English football. With Phillips and Niall Quinn leading the attack, Sunderland had two seventh place finishes in the Premiership before relegation in 2002.

As the club's patchy on the field performances again saw a period of fluctuation between the first and second tiers of English football, there were major changes off the field. Sir Bob Murray sold the club to Niall Quinn and his Drumaville Consortium of Irish investors in 2006 and then in 2008, the Drumaville Consortium sold the club to Irish-American billionaire Ellis Short.

A flurry of successive managers then flirted with relegation before finally succumbing in 2017, though fans thoroughly enjoyed a Capital One Cup Wembley appearance against Manchester City and a run of six consecutive victories against Newcastle. Despite the lack of relative success, attendance figures at the stadium have stayed high and the

love and affection for the Black Cats remains as strong as ever on Wearside. Hanging in the foyer of SAFC's magnificent Stadium of Light hangs one of the world's earliest football paintings. Thomas Marie Madawaska Hemy's 1895 Sunderland v Aston Villa picture (also known as A Corner Kick) portrays a match between the most successful English teams of the time. The match finished 4-4 and was played at the club's Newcastle Road ground.

Hemy (1837-1937) was born while his family were emigrating from Newcastle to Australia on the passenger ship SS Madawaska – hence one of his middle names. He returned to Tyneside later, studying at the Newcastle School of Art and later became a famed marine and coastal painter.

His most famous painting – other than the SAFC painting – is the Wreck of the Birkenhead, although he also painted Old Sunderland.

A long-standing rumour claimed Hemy had only portrayed boxers before painting the SAFC v Aston Villa game, hence every player and some onlookers have their fist clenched, is clearly untrue.

Almost a century after the Hemy painting, artist Chris Stevens became Artist in Residence at SAFC for the 1983-84 season. His work was later exhibited at the Northern Gallery for Contemporary Art in Sunderland and at the Glynn Vivian Gallery in Swansea.

Sunderland's Cultural Heritage

Whenever SAFC have been unable to provide entertainment, Wearsiders have long had the Sunderland Empire to turn to. The theatre is one of the biggest in the UK, the largest between Manchester and Edinburgh, and has over 1800 seats and a total capacity of 2,200. It opened for business in July 1907 and its distinctive 90ft tower has been a city icon and landmark ever since. Oscar winner Helen Mirren and Britain's first rock and roll singer Tommy Steele both made their stage debuts at the theatre, although it was on the Empire stage that on April 26, 1976, actor and Carry On star Sid James suffered a heat attack. He died on his way to hospital. His ghost, and that of Molly Moselle – a stage manager who disappeared from the theatre in 1949 – are said to haunt the backstage area. Originally known as the Empire Palace, the theatre was established by South Shields man Richard Thornton and opened with a packed performance by variety and vaudeville star Vesta Tilley, who had previously laid the foundation stone on September 29, 1906.

Thornton was an early pioneer of variety theatre and wanted to make the entertainment form more respectable, so he built the Empire as a palace, full of luxurious opulence. The theatre's main entrance was for the upper classes and well to do, while side entrances served the working classes. The Empire's dome originally had a revolving sphere topped by a seven-foot statute of the Greek muse of dance, Terpsichore, but these were removed during World War 2 after a German bomb exploded nearby. The statute now takes pride of place at the top of the Empire's grand staircase. In its early years, the Empire fared well, attracting large audiences to its programme of variety shows that included everything from cricketing elephants to cycling saxophonists.

Major stars of the time appeared, including W.C. Fields, Charlie Chaplin, Stan Laurel and Oliver Hardy, and Sir Harry Lauder. Later came appearances from Danny Kay, Morcambe and Wise, George Formby and The Beatles.

As touring theatre and the popularity of variety declined in the 1930s, the fortunes of the theatre waned, despite the introduction, in 1930, of moving pictures. The owners closed their Shields and Gateshead theatres, but the Empire survived. It also survived World War Two, when audiences swelled despite the city being a regular target of German bombers.

The growing popularity of television and the growing attraction of cinema led to a gradual decline and in May 1959, the Empire closed. It reopened the following year, having being bought for £52,000 by Sunderland Council, becoming the first 'number one' theatre in the UK under civic control.

Since then the Empire has been refurbished and re-equipped three times. In 1988 Billy Connolly was the star attraction of the re-opening of the Gallery area

In 2000 SFX took over its management on a 12-year contract. Later that year Clear Channel Entertainment (now Live Nation) bought SFX and four years later more than £4.5m was spent on a huge redevelopment project that enabled it to stage West End shows. The work enabled a new production of Miss Saigon to be performed in early 2005 and later in the same year, Chitty Chitty Bang Bang came to town. In its centenary year of 2007, the Empire hosted Starlight Express, The Producers, South Pacific and pantomime Cinderella, starring Hollywood legend Mickey Rooney. The Ambassador Theatre Group (ATG) now runs the Empire.

Rob Lawson

Many returning Wearsiders only consider themselves home once they've seen or passed Penshaw Monument. Officially the Earl of Durham's Monument, Penshaw Monument is a half-sized replica of the Temple of Hephaestus in Athens and was built in 1844. The folly is dedicated to John Lambton (1792-1844) 1st Earl of Durham and stands 66ft high (20m). The 5th Earl of Durham, John Lambton, gifted it to the National Trust in September 1939.

The monument is 30 metres long and 16 metres wide and was designed by father and son architects John and Benjamin Green, who also designed the popular Literary and Philosophical Society building in central Newcastle; the Theatre Royal, Newcastle; and Grey's Monument, also in Newcastle. Thomas Pratt of Sunderland built the monument. It is made of gritstone hewn from the Marquess of Londonderry's east coast quarries. Thomas Dundas, 2nd Earl of Zetland laid the foundation stone four years after the death of the 1st Earl of Durham on August 28, 1844

One of the monument's pillars enclosed a spiral staircase that gives access to the top of the structure. However, on Easter Monday 1926, teenager Temperley Arthur Scott was killed after falling from the monument. He and three friends had reached the roof via the staircase and were trying to avoid other visitors on the roof walkway when he fell through an area where there was no protecting wall. The staircase was closed to the public until August 29 2001 when controlled access was given so people could see the views from the monument. The exercise was a test to see how popular it would be – and more than 2,00 turned up. Regular weekend access is now available through the National Trust's website. The Wear splits Sunderland in two and river crossings have long been vital to the development of the city. The new Wear Bridge, which will link Wessington Way and Pallion, for example, will improve links between the A19, the city centre and the Port of Sunderland and is said to be a key part of the city's continuing regeneration. The new three-span, cable-stayed bridge will feature an A-frame pylon rising to 115m (379ft), twice as high as Gateshead's Millennium Bridge and taller than Big Ben. It will have two lanes of traffic in both directions, plus dedicated cycle ways and footpaths along its full length.

Rob Lawson

Further downstream, the Wearmouth Bridge is in its third reincarnation. The first opened in 1796 and was sponsored by Rowland Burdon MP. A plaque on the current bridge claims the original 'proved a catalyst for the growth of Sunderland.' It replaced a ferry service, with the nearest bridge being some way upstream at Chester-le-Street. Famous engineer Robert Stephenson was responsible for the reconstruction of the bridge between 1857 and 1859. The toll across the bridge was abolished a few years later in 1885. Work on the current bridge, built in response to the growing volume of traffic, began in 1927. It was built around the old one, allowing the road to remain to open during building work. The Duke of York, later King George VI, opened the new structure in October 1929.

The railway bridge, adjacent to the Wearmouth Bridge, was built in 1879, while the impressive Queen Alexandra Bridge, further upstream, opened in 1909. The Hylton Bridge, carrying the A19 from South Hylton to North Hylton was opened in 1974. The New Wear Crossing will open in 2018, standing 105m (344ft) high it is twice the height of Nelson's column and will open up a wide area of Wearside for economic development.

Three years before the Hylton Bridge's completion, the city had lost one of its most famous landmarks. The decision to demolish Sunderland's old town hall still angers and frustrates Wearsiders to this day. The striking building, built in a French-inspired classical style with a large clock tower, dominated Fawcett Street from the time it opened to its demolition in 1971. In truth, it was already too small for a thriving, ambitious town when it opened in 1890 and people who worked there complained about noise from the busy railway station behind and Fawcett Street in front.

Rob Lawson

Sunderland's Cultural Heritage

Just next to the old town hall stood another Sunderland landmark, very much part of the city's heritage. Yorkshireman George Binns had established a drapery business in the city in 1807. George's son Henry grew the business, trading under his own name. The business grew steadily, staying in the Binns family and moving several times to larger premises. By the start of the First World War, Binns was trading on both sides of Fawcett Street and was the city's largest department store. In 1953 Binns became part of the House of Fraser retail empire and its Sunderland stores were rebuilt and refurbished in 1962 and then 1972. By the 1980s, however, the store was struggling and departments closed. It finally closed in 1993. Its old retail rival, Joplings lasted longer. James Jopling had established the store in High Street West in 1804. By the 1950s, Joplings had become a limited company and employed more than 500 people. However, in December 1954 the store was burned to the ground in a huge fire that destroyed the store and all of its contents. After trading from a temporary base at the old High Street site, a new four-storey department store opened in 1956 on John Street. Despite the closure of

Street was conceived as a residential street, but by the late 19th century it was the heart of the town's commercial and shopping sector. By this point the town had followed the Victorian tradition for large, open public places – parks. Sunderland council had purchased old quarrying land close to what is now the city centre from the wealthy Mowbray family. Mowbray Park was opened in 1857. The grand park has several Victorian monuments, the most poignant of which is that to the memory of the Victoria Hall disaster. The monument is close to the Toward Road site of Victoria Hall, where on June 16, 1883 183 children died after panic in the theatre led to a catastrophic crush. Excited youngsters from an upper tier had rushed to a lower tier to get free treats that were being thrown into the audience from the performers. They were caught up against a door that would only open one way. The tragedy prompted a worldwide change in public arena safety measures – the pre-cursor to modern-day fire doors. A German parachute bomb destroyed the Victoria Hall in 1941.

Another Mowbray Park monument is a sculpture

"It was a bustling, thriving town, with a growing number of successful middle and upper class families who were making their fortunes"

its rival Binns, Joplings too began to struggle in the 1980s and 1990s. Changes of ownership couldn't stem the decline and it closed its doors for the last time in June 2010. The size and stature of both stores when they opened in the early years of the 19th century are an indication of the pre-eminence of Sunderland at that time. It was a bustling, thriving town, with a growing number of successful middle and upper class families who were making their fortunes through Wearside's three main industries – shipbuilding, coalmining and glass production. There were plenty of jobs for the town's working classes, and as the Victorian era heralded the Industrial Revolution, more and more people from the surrounding areas and beyond signed up into its coalmines, shipyards and factories.

Areas like Sunniside, John Street and Athenaeum Street still have the Victorian terraces built for the town's middle classes.

Earlier, the opening of the first Wearmouth Bridge had been a catalyst for growth and Fawcett Street, built on land belonging to landowner Christopher Fawcett, had been constructed, leading south from High Street. Fawcett

of a walrus. This huge artwork commemorates Alice in Wonderland author Lewis Carroll and his poem, the Walrus and the Carpenter. Lewis Carroll was a regular visitor to nearby Whitburn, as well as Sunderland. Carroll's sisters Elizabeth and Mary lived in Southwick after the latter married local vicar, the Reverend Charles Collingwood.

But perhaps the most famous Victorian memorial in Mowbray Park is that to Sunderland sailor hero Jack Crawford. Jack died in 1831, but was a national figure thanks to his bravery 34 years earlier. Born into Sunderland's East End, or Old Sunderland, Jack worked as a keelman before being pressganged into the Royal Navy in 1796. A year later, on October 11, 1797, the Navy fought the Battle of Camperdown off the coast of Holland against the Dutch navy. Jack was serving on The Venerable, the flagship of the fleet commander Admiral Duncan, when its mast and flag were shot down. The lowering of the flag signified surrender, so young Jack climbed the remains of the mast and nailed the flag back into place. He did so under intense fire from the Dutch – one bullet pierced his cheek. Victory followed

and Jack was hailed a national hero. Jack's bravery is believed to have given rise to the phrase "nailing your colours to the mast." Sadly, Jack fell on hard times and was often to be found drunk. He was one of the first victims of the cholera epidemic that struck in 1831.

At the northern end of Mowbray Park stands a symbol of the town's Victorian wealth, the Sunderland Museum and Winter Gardens. The museum, the first publicly run outside of London, was opened in 1879. Sir Samuel Storey who was the town's mayor, the town's MP and the founder in 1873 of the Sunderland Echo, laid its first stone. American Civil War hero and recently retired US President Ulysses S Grant was in attendance. Attached to the museum were the Winter Gardens, a large glasshouse fashioned on London's Crystal Palace.

As the town's shipbuilders prospered, so the town grew. The Edwardian period saw Sunderland's importance as a centre for shipbuilding reach its peak. It is estimated that during the 30 years leading up to the First World War, one in three of ships built across the world was constructed in the north east yards – with Sunderland being the undisputed foremost shipbuilding town.

In the early Edwardian years, the industry accounted for up to 40 per cent of the male labour force and had created employment for the masses and huge wealth for a few. Sunderland was a confident, affluent, optimistic town and this was reflected in grand buildings being constructed – the Empire, for instance. Sunderland historian Tom Corfe said: "The Edwardian decade placed an architectural crown upon Sunderland's century of growth".

These also saw the construction of the Queen Alexandra Bridge, the town's first electric trams, which helped stimulate growth out to Sunderland suburbs, and the introduction of electric street lighting. The city can be particularly proud of the last innovation, as it was a Sunderland man, Joseph Swann, who had invented the electric light bulb in 1878.

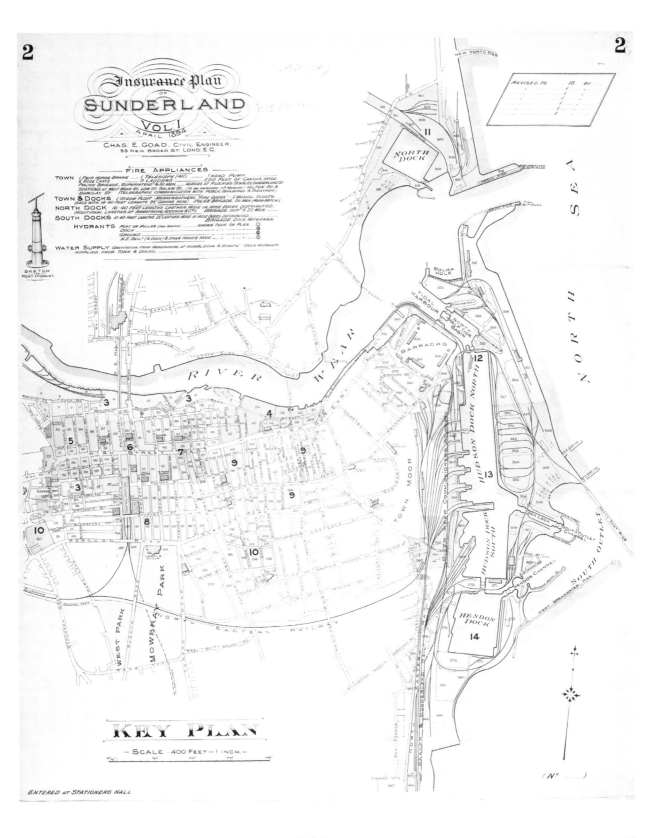

Innovation was key to a major new development on the Sunderland coastline. Roker Pier and Lighthouse, Sunderland's most photographed structure, was built between 1885 and 1903 and the Grade II listed complex was hailed as a 'triumph of engineering' upon completion. It was the brainchild of one man – Henry Wake, chief engineer of the River Wear Commissioners, an elected body of local mine owners, landowners, merchants and shipowners who controlled and financed the development of the docks and harbour until the creation of the Port of Sunderland Authority in 1973.

Sunderland at the end of the 19th century had grown into one of the biggest and most important coal shipping ports in the country, but the original harbour was more than a century old and incapable of sustaining the export of 15,000 tons of coal a day. It was proposed that a new outer harbour would be built at the mouth of the Wear, protecting the old, crumbling inner harbour breakwaters that had been built in the mid 18th century. More than 125 acres of safe water for shipping would be created in the process.

The proposal also allowed for the creation of a new lighthouse. The old breakwaters – which survive as the old North and South Piers – each had a lighthouse. The white lighthouse that now stands proud in Roker Cliff Park originally stood on the South Pier, from where it was deactivated in 1903 and removed 80 years later.

The foundation stone for the new Roker Pier – the north arm of the harbour – was laid in September 1885. Wake solved a huge array of logistical and engineering problems with new innovative techniques and equipment, and the pier began to inch 2000ft out to sea. It was made of granite-faced blocks weighing up to 45 tons that were constructed in the area now called the Blockyard. The crane known as Goliath which moved these enormous blocks was designed and built by Wake and powered by gas engines that were supplied by gas pipes that ran the length of the pier's internal tunnel. The lighthouse was built in 1902 and stands 138ft high. The grey and red Aberdeen granite used in its construction was a clever way of incorporating the traditional red and white stripes used in lighthouse design without incurring long-term maintenance and painting costs. It is claimed that the lighthouse's original lantern could be seen up to 15 miles out to sea. It was gas powered and emitted a 45,000 candlepower reflected beam.

The pier and lighthouse took more than 18 years to complete and was eventually opened on September 23, 1903 amid much ceremony.

The new South Pier was started at about the same time as the North Pier, but construction work was halted by the outbreak of the First World War. It was never fully completed and the new twin lighthouse never built.

A tunnel beneath the North Pier (Roker Pier) that originally carried gas pipes for the Goliath crane, was used by the lighthouse keeper in bad weather.

The complex has recently undergone a multi-million pound restoration programme, jointly funded by Sunderland City Council and the Heritage Lottery Fund. This work includes the restoration of the lighthouse interior, repair of the tunnel floor and drains, and the improvement of access. The final phase will be to build a new entrance structure, with a view to opening the structure to the public for the first time in the pier's 112-year history, the tunnel linking Sunderland's future to its proud past.

Rob Lawson

Sunderland's Industrial Heritage

Washington F Pit

It is rare to find a colliery building still standing in the North East, even though they were once a very common sight. One that can still be seen today is the F Pit in Washington, now a mining museum. The pits belonging to Washington Colliery were given letters instead of proper names, so there was Washington A Pit, B Pit, C Pit, D Pit, E Pit, H Pit, and I Pit, but only the F Pit building survives. The F Pit opened back in 1777 but the present engine house only dates from the early twentieth century. An underground explosion in 1796, meant the pit was abandoned for a while, but it re-opened again in 1820. F pit was deep with the bottom seam of coal being 113 fathoms or 200meters underground in 1894. The colliery produced coal throughout the first half of the twentieth century. By the 1950s there were more than 1,500 miners employed there, and the pit produced half a million tonnes of coal every year. It was finally closed by the National Coal Board in 1968. Fortunately, the engine house was preserved as a fitting monument to have in the new town of Washington and it eventually became a museum in 1976 and is a wonderful reminder of Washington's mining past.

Ryhope Engines Museum

In 1864, the industrial revolution was gathering pace in Britain and Sunderland was at the very forefront of this shift, but a growing town was also a thirsty town and also need clean water to prevent the spread of disease. The Sunderland and South Shields Water Company, the water suppliers to Sunderland at the time, were aware that they needed to increase the water supply to the town in order to keep up with rising demand. So, that same year, the company bought four acres of land in Ryhope, and the following May, Thomas Hawksley was tasked with designing a pumping station which would quench the thirst of the Sunderland people - he subsequently produced the designs for what became The Ryhope Pumping Station. The two engines which were responsible for pumping the water in Hawksley's new station are massive, each of them having a beam weighing 22 tons and a flywheel weighing 18 tons; the beams having to be supported 22 feet in the air as they rock back and forth.

The entire project was a massive undertaking, which in the end cost the Company £58,418 (equivalent to almost £2,700,000 today) but it was worth it. Clean water was pumped from the magnesian limestone rock beneath Ryhope and transferred straight into the homes and businesses of people in Sunderland. The Ryhope Pumping Station eventually closed in 1967 after a century of use, and has been turned into Ryhope Engines Museum, a monument to Sunderland's industrial heritage.

Richard Callaghan

Monkwearmouth Station

Monkwearmouth Station was described by the famous architectural historian Nikolaus Pevsner as "one of the most handsome stations in existence". It is still handsome today but no longer used as a terminus for trains. It was built in 1848 by a local architect called Thomas Moore for the railway businessman George Hudson. Hudson was known as the 'Railway King' and was the MP for Sunderland. He built railways and stations all over the country but wanted to have a particularly grand station for the town which he represented in Parliament. Sadly, the station closed in 1967. Trains still go through the station on the way to Sunderland station, although they no longer stop here. For some time it was a railway museum but has now become the Sunderland AFC Fans Museum. The brainchild and lifelong love of Sunderland Fan, Michael Ganley, it holds not only a huge collection of SAFC memorabilia but also items from all over the whole world of football allowing every football fan to take a trip down memory lane.

Richard Callaghan

National Glass Centre

WORDS BY *Keith Merrin and Julia Stephenson*
National Glass Centre

National Glass Centre

"Sunderland's association with glass dates back to the year 674 AD"

It is believed that the first glass making in Britain happened during the Bronze Age (2500 – 800 BC) when small simple objects like glass beads were made. During the Roman occupation (43 – 410 AD) glassware was imported from Europe and North Africa. While Sunderland cannot claim to have introduced glass to Britain, the region and the Wearmouth area in particular, has a history in glass dating back to the seventh century. From this point onwards glass has played an important role in supporting employment, international trade and reputation and education.

Sunderland's association with glass production dates back to the year 674 AD when Benedict Biscop founded the monastery on the site that we now think of as St Peter's Church. Following one of a number of trips to Rome, Biscop returned to Wearmouth with glassmakers from France who shared their skills and created a coloured glass window for the monastery. This was the first recorded use of coloured glass in Britain.

From around 1600, glassmakers from Northern Europe began to move to Britain to meet growing demand from the wealthy for glass. These glassmakers belonged to groups of people including the Huguenots who came to Britain to escape religious persecution. The focus on glass production in the North East grew during the reign of James I (1566 – 1625). The monarch prioritised the use of timber for ship-building and banned its use as a fuel for glassmaking. Coal was the obvious alternative and Sir Robert Mansell, Admiral of the Royal Navy and Member of Parliament, recognised the potential of the North East's cheap coal supply. By 1623 Mansell had bought full rights to glass making in Tyneside and had become the exclusive producer of glass in England. Following the end of the English Civil War production was taken over by a Guild of Glassmakers who prevented the establishment of any new glass industry in Tyneside. In response to this restriction the Sunderland Company of Glassmakers was formed by ten business men and by 1696 three glassworks had been established in Sunderland, at Ayres Quay, Deptford making bottles, at Southwick making bottles and window glass and at Bishopwearmouth Pans making tableware.

During the eighteenth century North East England was acknowledged as an ideal region for glass manufacturer. Not only was coal readily available, the cheapest coal that would otherwise be burnt away at the pit-head could be used to heat glass furnaces. Good shipping routes were also established between the North East, London and the Baltic, the ships used sand as ballast and sand is a key ingredient required to make glass.

In 1836 the Wear Glassworks was established by John & James Hartley. The company became best known as Hartley Wood (later Sunderland Glassworks) and was in operation, in Sunderland, until 2000. By 1838 James Hartley had developed a new method for making sheet glass and was granted a patent. This new approach requiring glass to be ladled onto a table, rolled out then polished creating strong and affordable glass that could be used for skylights and roofs used by factories and railway stations. James Chance of Birmingham bought the licence to use to use the technique in order to build the Crystal Palace for the Great Exhibition of 1851. James Hartley's method was used to create sheet glass

until 1952 when Alistair Pilkington invented a new process for mass-producing high quality flat glass.

In 1895 James Hartley Jnr. (grandson of the founder) went into partnership with the colour mixer Alfred Wood and the company gained an international reputation for the quality of their coloured glass.

Another company that would take glass production in Sunderland from strength to strength and into the twentieth century was formed as Angus and Greener in 1858 by Henry Greener and James Angus. The company specialised in pressed glass using a technique developed in America. This technique supported the production of affordable decorative domestic glass. In 1921 the company became James A. Jobling & Co. In this year the company secured the patent rights from the American company Corning Inc. to produce Pyrex. Joblings supplied Pyrex glass to every country in the British Commonwealth (with the exception of Canada) and at its height produced approximately 30 million pieces of glass a year and exported to 120 countries.

During the second half of the twentieth century artists working predominantly in Scandinavia, Czechoslovakia (now the Czech Republic), Germany and the United States began to explore how glass could be used in their work. Of course there were artists before them, most notably

National Glass Centre

Émile Gallé and René Lalique, whose outstanding practice in glass had international impact, however, it was artists including Stanislav Libenský and Jaroslava Brychtová (Czech), Erwin and Gretel Eisch (Bavaria) and Harvey Littleton (USA) who pioneered the Studio Glass Movement from the 1950s onwards. From the outset of the Movement these artists taught and shared their skills leading to the establishment of a number of courses teaching artists to work in glass.

In the late 1960s, Charles Bray who taught at Sunderland's Teacher Training College, (an organisation that would ultimately become part of the University of Sunderland) was asked to teach a course on ceramic glazes and glass. Having no prior knowledge of glass Bray worked with John Stirling, a previous employee of Jobling and lecturer in Post- Graduate Glass Physics at Sunderland Polytechnic, to prepare a course. This experience would be the start of his long-term passion for glass.

Through the 1960s and 70s Charles Bray worked with Sunderland's glass industry to support the establishment of glass within the educational curriculum. He developed

"National Glass Centre opened in 1998"

contacts in Scandanavia, France and Germany developing an interest in and reputation for glass in Sunderland. He also established facilities for glass making at Monkwearmouth College and a programme of residencies for artists working in glass. By 1982 Charles Bray had established a BA (Hons) course in 3D Design Glass with Ceramics. He chose to leave academic life at this point to pursue his own practice and the Swedish artist Göran Wärff became the first course leader. Although industrial production of glass in Sunderland had gone into decline by the end of the twentieth century, the work of Charles Bray and his associates established a new path for glass to follow in Sunderland.

By the mid 1990s the growing department at what was now the University of Sunderland became involved in the planning stages for National Glass Centre. With support from the Tyne & Wear Development Corporation and the first major arts lottery award in the North East, National Glass Centre opened in 1998. The building incorporated significant facilities for glass making, at first used by Hartley Wood (by this time known as Sunderland Glass Works),

"National Glass Centre's exhibition programme presents the highest standard of artists' work in glass and supports the development of the best new practice"

a hot glass studio demonstrating glass blowing to the visiting public, artist studio spaces, galleries, facilities for public engagement, a shop, a café and spaces for corporate hire. In 2000 the Glass & Ceramics Department of the University of Sunderland took over the facilities previously used by Hartley Wood and in 2010 the University took over the full governance of National Glass Centre. Following investment from the University, Arts Council England, Heritage Lottery Fund, The James Knott Trust and The Gillian Dickinson Trust National Glass Centre re-launched in Summer 2013.

In the three full academic years following re-launch in 2013, National Glass Centre has welcomed an average of 219,393 visitors per year and worked with an average of 58 Foundation Art & Design/Extended students, 62 Glass and Ceramics BA (Hons) students, 15 MA Glass and Ceramics students and 19 PhD students per year.

National Glass Centre's exhibition programme presents the highest standard of artist's work in glass, supports the development of the best new practice and enhances our visitor's experience and enjoyment. Recent exhibitions include a retrospective of the work of Erwin Eisch, one

of the founders of the Studio Glass Movement, a series of installations by Magdalene Odundo, an artist renowned for her ceramics who worked at National Glass Centre to explore the potential of glass within her practice and the dynamic work of the Mexican De La Torre Brothers.

With the skill of National Glass Centre's staff and the access to glass making equipment, the Centre is able to operate as so much more than a gallery presenting finished art-work. Much of the work shown in the gallery is made in our studios, artists of international reputation visit sharing their skills with students and the visiting public, established artists looking to explore the potential of the material come to work with the guidance of our team and we offer regular residencies to artists in the early stages of their careers. In recent years artists who have worked at National Glass Centre include, Katharine Dowson, Bruce McLean, William Tillyer, Gijs Bakker, Magdalene Odundo, Richard Slee, Martin Janecky and David King.

National Glass Centre benefits greatly from national and international partnership working including ongoing support from staff at the Victoria & Albert Museum. Following the

Keith Merrin and Julia Stephenson

re-launch in 2013 National Glass Centre has worked with a different organisation each year loaning and displaying works from collections held by National Museums of Scotland (The Dan Klein & Alan J. Poole Private Collection) in 2013/14, North Lands Creative Glass, in 2014/15, Tacoma Museum of Glass in 2015/16 and Ebletoft Glass Museum in 2016/17. The programme of collection loans has acted as an introduction between organisations and long-term partnership working is underway allowing the sharing of exhibitions and good practice in all areas of National Glass Centre's work.

National Glass Centre has recently decided to develop a formal collection. By acquiring work created by artists who exhibit with us or undertake residencies we have the opportunity to build an exemplary permanent collection of the finest examples of contemporary practice in international glass

Our public learning and engagement programme reaches an average of 7,115 people per year. We offer a programme for school groups, families and adults as well as focussed projects. For example, with support from the Esme Fairbairn Foundation, National Glass Centre delivered a six-month project in 2015 for people living with dementia and their carers. Participants met on a weekly basis undertaking creative projects in glass led by an artist. The project culminated in an exhibition of the artwork created and has led to the delivery of a similar project at National Glass Centre beginning in early 2016. This project is being delivered in collaboration with Equal Arts over a period of eighteen months.

National Glass Centre has established a partnership with Forward Assist, a charity offering support to veterans facing a range of issues connected with adjusting to civilian life. Over the last year the group has undertaken three projects learning glassmaking and drawing skills.

Keith Merrin and Julia Stephenson

National Glass Centre

"Our public learning and engagement programme reaches an average of 7,115 people per year. We offer a programme for school groups, families and adults as well as focused projects"

One participant Pat, who served in the Navy for 22 years, said: "I had a wonderful experience finding out the concepts of how glass is transformed into the fantastic pieces that were created during our time with National Glass Centre staff. I felt that I had learnt so much during my time with the project and with the help and support of the staff we were able to achieve that. The whole experience was self-satisfying and I felt proud of myself for being able absorb all that was shown and taught to us. So a Big thank you to all that were involved in the project."

National Glass Centre is now in its third year of involvement in the Sorrell Foundation's National Art & Design Saturday Club. The scheme aims to encourage young people aged between 14-16 to consider the potential of careers in the creative industries. Approximately twenty young people attend National Glass Centre every term-time Saturday morning for one year where they work with our academic staff learning new skills and techniques in art including ceramics, print and working with hot glass. In the Autumn term they join other young people from across the country who are involved in the scheme in London where they visit National Museums and Galleries. In the Spring term they undertake a Master Class with a notable artist and in the Summer term they rejoin their national peers in London to exhibit their work at Somerset House. National Glass Centre also presents an annual exhibition of the work created by the young people.

With support from Youth Music, National Glass Centre delivered a project titled 'Glass Beats'. This project created an opportunity for a number of young people with additional educational needs, and others who had experienced social disadvantage, to take part in a project combining art and music. The young people worked with artists to create musical instruments in glass and ceramics. Working with a musician, the young people performed their music in front of an audience at St Peter's Church. A number of the young people achieved their Bronze Arts Award through participation in the project. The instruments and a film of the performance formed the basis of an exhibition at National Glass Centre

The projects outlined above rely heavily on the skills of artists who are able to work with a wide range of people. Working with Barbican, National Glass Centre is currently delivering an Art Works Fellowship programme supporting two regional artists. Effie Burns and Sue Woolhouse have received investment to allow them to develop their own practice with a view to enhancing their offer when they work with the public.

National Glass Centre looks forward to playing a key role in Sunderland's cultural development supporting artists and promoting the City of Sunderland and the North East region.

Sunderland's Magnificent Coastline

Roker and Seaburn

Boasting Sunderland's two beautiful beaches, for many decades Roker and Seaburn were favourite holiday destinations for people from Sunderland, Wearside and around the North East. Development in Roker began in 1587 when the Abbs family were granted land on the north side of the river on the proviso that they supplied six soldiers for the defence of the mouth of the river.

At this point, what we now know as Sunderland was divided into three quite distinct settlements, Bishopwearmouth in the west, Sunderland in the east, and Monkwearmouth to the north of the river. Over the succeeding centuries, the area north of the river saw more growth, whilst still remaining a distinct village of its own.

By the late eighteenth century, the growth of all three villages had seen them begin to combine into a larger town. The construction of the first Wearmouth Bridge in 1796, the second iron bridge in the world, accelerated this process whilst giving the people of Sunderland significantly easier access to the beaches on the north side of the Wear.

The Borough of Sunderland was created in 1835, but it wasn't until 1897 that Monkwearmouth was officially absorbed into the town.

In 1898 Roker became home to Sunderland AFC, Roker Park the club's sixth ground after leaving Newcastle Road. Roker Park was to be Sunderland's home stadium for almost a century, until the 1997 move to the Stadium of Light.

The area has stunning beaches and magnificent views and is often forgotten by those who see Sunderland as an industrial city. It is currently undergoing considerable redevelopment with significant investment from both the public and private sectors, reaffirming Sunderland's proud claim to be 'the City by the Sea'.

Roker Pier

Construction of Roker Pier began on September 14, 1885. It followed the passage of an Act of Parliament in 1883 sanctioning the construction of a new North Pier, now known as Roker Pier. Sir James Laing, Chairman of the River Wear Commissioners, laid the foundation stone of a pier that was regarded at the time as a marvel of modern engineering. 2,000 feet long, the granite faced concrete blocks making up the pier were placed using a gas-powered crane nicknamed 'Goliath'.

The Pier, built to protect Sunderland's thriving harbour and port, replaced an earlier pier constructed between 1786 and 1796. The construction of the new pier came during a period of growth for Sunderland, with Monkwearmouth becoming part of the city in 1897.

Roker Pier was completed in 1903, with a lighthouse at its tip constructed from naturally coloured red and white Aberdeen granite. When constructed, Roker Lighthouse was the most powerful port lighthouse in Britain.

Roker Pier and Lighthouse were given Grade II listing in 1994 in recognition of the pier's special historic significance. In 2012, Sunderland City Council began a programme of restoration to the pier and lighthouse, with work completed in 2016.

The pier has stood proudly at the mouth of the River Wear both as a symbol of Sunderland's maritime heritage and as a light to guide visiting ships safely to harbour in the Port of Sunderland.

Sunderland's Magnificent Coastline

The Visual Arts In Sunderland

WORDS BY *Alistair Robinson*
Programme Director, Northern Gallery
for Contemporary Art

The Visual Arts In Sunderland

"In 1980, the magazine Artists' Newsletter was founded to give artists a voice"

The history of art works in mysterious ways. It isn't quite as told by the victors, as is said about history with a large H, although it might seem like that. Rather, it's told about two things: proximity, both socially to those in positions of power and geographically to journals of record, and the desire to historicize a city or region's cultural contribution. It came as a surprise to me when first moving to North-East England that much of what passes for standard operating procedure or else 'best practice' in the visual arts in England started life as an idea first formulated in and around Sunderland, or some other part of the North-East at some point in the last forty years.

On my first visit to the Museum of Modern Art, New York, back in the last millennium, the only artworks by British artists on show in the entire building were by photographers, all working in the 1980s. No sculpture, no painting, no installation, performance, no Young British Artists (then at the height of their fame). But there were photographs of Sunderland, much to my then total disbelief. There was one room allocated to British artists out of around fifty: Britain's place in the artistic world, much to my surprise, was of minor consequence to our transatlantic cousins. But the one room had sights of astonishing beauty and squalor: the images burned into my retina. One series was Paul Graham's series A1: The Great North Road, which featured images of northern England at Blyth, Rainton and Newcastle, and Berwick, that seemed as though they had been shot earlier that day – or a thousand years ago. More arrestingly still, Chris Killip's extraordinary photographs of Sunderland, such as MoMA's Untitled (1988), came as a revelation. Killip is now a Professor at Harvard University, though he has Sunderland to thank for his worldly success. Killip carried around a 10x8" plate camera to punk gigs and found a subculture – a world, we might say – that no one else could have. To have captured the energy, raw anger, and consummate chaos of that subculture was an achievement – to have done so upon the most unwieldy camera known to humanity, that was able to transform anger into beauty, chaos into exquisitely organized compositions – was beyond that. Both the Victoria & Albert Museum, where I worked later, and the Museum of Modern Art, had bought work from this artist who found his milieu in Sunderland. Other histories do exist.

Slightly earlier, in 1980, the magazine Artists' Newsletter was founded to give artists a voice in how they wanted their own work to be discussed and known. At the back of the magazine there was a forum for finding commissions, exhibitions, and other opportunities. Up until that point, most writing about living artists was by Courtauld Institute and Oxbridge-educated art historians. They have their virtues: I am one. And they have their weaknesses: most had never had to make a living in the way artists do – by throwing their ideas out to their peers and to the public and hoping not to be humiliated, and hoping that they could pay the rent, month after month after month. Almost none of the critics at that point worked outside of London. (A fair few, then as now, had scarcely set foot outside of London.) Something began to change in 1980, though, with the arrival of Artists' Newsletter as a means of self- organisation. Artists could be taken seriously as interpreters of their own and of their peers' work. In the US that had been the case for decades, as the

magazine Artforum published artists' writings in the 1960s. In England, the struggle to catch up, and the move for artists to have a public voice of their own that was also a debating platform, began in Sunderland, in part.

Earlier still, back in 1972, there was a vision to convert a former set of farm buildings and a barn into a space for art and artists. That became what is today Arts Centre Washington. Washington is a new town between Sunderland and Newcastle, and now part of the former. Almost entirely without precedence, the venue became "a hotbed of radical video art" according to the art historian and curator Dawn Bothwell, whose pioneering work on rediscovering the art of that period is now the subject of her doctoral research. That period now seems far away – but the ambitions and ideals that motivated the small group of individuals who created pioneering ways of working now live on.

Such high ambitions live on for example in the artist-run group CIRCA, run by two University of Sunderland graduates and one Sunderland doctoral researcher. CIRCA have shown artists from across the world, given people their first opportunity to exhibit in the UK since organising their first exhibitions in the remarkably beautiful Grade I listed Holy Trinity church in Sunderland's east end. On freezing winter evenings, in one of the most handsome parish churches in England, UK audiences were introduced to the world premieres of artworks by UK artists, and UK premieres

"The city is also, perhaps surprisingly, continuing to exert a fascination for artists."

by artists from around the world. The figures CIRCA have brought to Sunderland (and to Britain) include acclaimed figures such as Clemens von Wedemeyer and Mario Pfeiffer, as well as British artists including Ed Atkins and Eric Bainbridge. It may still strike some as odd, perhaps, that an artist of international repute such as Von Wedemeyer should have his first UK solo show in Sunderland. Stranger things have happened. There is a sense, amongst many in Sunderland that anything is possible – if one has the ingenuity and the guile to make it happen. The 'art world' operates, in many respects, as a pack, with rather more following and rather fewer leading, and fewer still willing to pursue their own route into the world. That spirit of adventure that CIRCA have shown is not merely exceptional in northern England: theirs is a programme that any city or region in the world would be delighted to have. Naturally enough, as this is Sunderland we are talking about, one of the three members of CIRCA commutes between the city and Dusseldorf – continuing the commitment to a cosmopolitan internationalism that predecessors in the 1970s and 1980s had pioneered.

The story of the visual arts in Sunderland has yet to be written. Bothwell's research will make a contribution to this history. But one thing is clear: with a handful of visionary individuals, a small amount of money, and boundless ambition, history can be made. At which point we need to correct ourselves: history wasn't made – news was. The history is still missing. Most of the time, my predecessors as curators were far too busy organising exhibitions, publishing extravagantly designed books, and forging new connections around the world to stop to historicize their own work. No one stopped to record the amazing activities that were fostered in Sunderland in the 1970s, 1980s and 1990s. The process of telling that story is only beginning to happen now, with people acting as archaeologists in the archives.

The city is also, perhaps surprisingly, continuing to exert a fascination for artists. The extraordinary film-maker Joanna Hogg, who has produced three of the most inspiring British-made films of the last decade, Exhibition, Unrelated, and Archipelago, is basing her next film, 'The Souvenir' on her time in the city, set circa 1980. The timing is done with good

reason. At that time, Ceolfrith Arts Centre, which became Northern Centre for Contemporary Art, and then Northern Gallery for Contemporary Art, was one of the most vibrant galleries – and publishing houses, and poetry bookshops – anywhere in the UK. In 1980 Hogg visited Sunderland as the guest of a famous artist staging a solo exhibition at the gallery. And she stayed for the best part of a year, entranced by the sights. After the Thatcher years, the impression can easily be had that creativity and inspiration are confined to glamorous postcodes. The truth is, of course, that creativity can flourish fully when it is given the space and opportunity to do so. Sunderland has furnished artists, writers and curators with the possibility of doing something that could and would not be done anywhere else.

Since the 1990s, the new media historian and curator Professor Beryl Graham, based at the University of Sunderland as part of the unit CRUMB, has waged a campaign to celebrate and document the creativity unleashed by the digital revolution. As she and many colleagues have written, in England some of the strongest forms of support for new ideas and new ways of working have not come from the largest institutions, or the richest cities, but from what appear to be the margins, geographically or financially. Graham's world-leading work has been published by MIT Press, in one of the richest universities on the planet some three thousand miles away (MIT has an investment fund of $1.5 billion at the time of writing, which even Oxford colleges can only look upon with envy). Along with a few others, she has ensured that there genuinely is now something approaching a shared history of artists' work made using digital technologies. Again, that this came out of Sunderland should come as no surprise: such work could not have been achieved from 'older' universities with more fossilised disciplinary and departmental structures, and a less open attitude towards new ways of thinking. We might say that the world has caught up with Graham, eventually: CRUMB began life around the millennium. In 2016, some of the artists that she and colleagues have so vigorously championed are now represented in the permanent collections of Tate and The Museum of Modern Art, New York, among many other places.

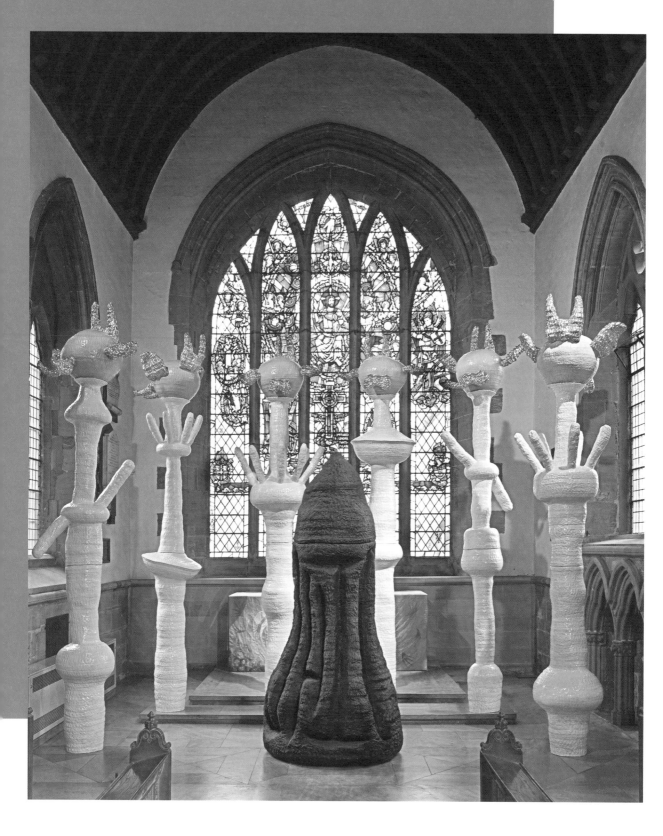

The Visual Arts In Sunderland

Eventually the avant-garde becomes accepted as part of the establishment, as so often happens. But that which is avant-garde first found support in adventurous, cosmopolitan, outward-looking places that cared less for other peoples' opinions than for running with inspired hunches and placing their trust in what they believed to be the art of the future.

Which brings me to Northern Gallery for Contemporary Art. Over roughly the same time period that Graham has been based in Sunderland, Northern Gallery for Contemporary Art (NGCA) has similarly brought people to public attention long before sister venues in the country managed to secure their talents. In this, there are many precedents, as we have seen above. NGCA awarded the film-maker and photographer Sam Taylor-Wood (now Taylor-Johnson) with her first large-scale public commission, and publication, back in 1996; the performance artist Lali Chetwynd (now Marvin Gaye Chetwynd) with her first public exhibition in 2003; the socially engaged artist Ruth Ewan in 2006, the ingenious Simon Martin not long after, amongst many others. The gallery brought the filmmaker

Such things couldn't happen today of course – except for when they could. In 2007, NGCA commissioned the Danish designer Mathias Bengtsson to create a new type of sculptural design – in fact the world's lightest seating system, created entirely from carbon fibre. One of the resulting works was acquired by The Museum of Modern Art. The travel of ideas this time was from SR1 to NY10019. Similarly, in 2009 the gallery commissioned the New York- based digital artist and musician Cory Arcangel to create a new work. Fast-forward several years: Tate bought the work and has shown it in Tate Modern. This time, the work has travelled from SR1 to SE1, and been seen by hundreds of thousands of people from all over the world. It was our faith in artists that allowed that to happen.

Also in 2009, the gallery gave the young artist-photographer Natasha Caruana her first ever opportunity in a public space, commissioning a large-scale body of work called Married Man. In 2016 it is being shown in the International Centre for Photography's new building as part of their inaugural exhibition; it then tours to Dallas. Again, SR1 to

"Finally, though, history catches up with us. NGCA has been one of the leading exhibition galleries in the country for fifty years"

Harun Farocki to the UK for the first time, in 2008 – some six years before Tate bought a work and larger London- based galleries took notice. In Sunderland, it seems, it's acceptable – desirable, in fact – to take a risk, and follow one's faith in art whatever others think. It's our job to find the next generation of talent and to support it, whether that talent lives in the city or far further afield. We have a long track record in this – and it has paid dividends over time.

In 1981, two brilliant curators called Peter Davies, and Chris Carrell, at Northern Centre for Contemporary Art, NGCA's predecessor – organised an exhibition of painters from North America called Who Chicago? This gave British audiences the first chance to see a whole range of work from across the Atlantic that had been gaining attention worldwide. That exhibition toured both to Camden Arts Centre in Hampstead and to the Serpentine Gallery in Kensington. In 1987, NGCA toured another exhibition, of work by American artist Claes Oldenburg, again to the Serpentine gallery. The trajectory of ideas was, in postcode terms, from SR2 to SW7: from the post-industrial north to Kensington Gardens. Art's history has a strange way of forgetting such things.

NY10036, then on to TX 75201. In 2015 she was one of only two female artists in the Arles photography festival, the world's most important celebration of photography. But you had to be in Sunderland to see her first.

Finally, though, history catches up with us. NGCA has been one of the leading exhibition galleries in the country for fifty years, under different guises and names. Until very recently, my predecessors and myself were too busy to stop acting and start thinking, if the truth is told. Artists and others had been making breaking news in Sunderland – but we hadn't been making history. You may have noticed a pattern, above. A small number of people, myself included, had brought fifteen Turner Prize nominees to the city (all before they were nominated, obviously), and innumerable international artists. We had spotted and supported the talent under our noses: Tim Brennan, Eric Bainbridge, Sophie Lisa Beresford, Lothar Goetz, and many others. Unlike in other continental European countries, we didn't found a museum of all the works we had helped to make or to show. And at the time of writing, that is changing, and changing fast. The whole landscape of arts funding across England is being transformed: and some of the clearest thinking about how we can address the major challenges of the near future is still coming out of Sunderland.

Until recently, it was so simple: galleries showed and helped create artworks, museums collected them, and universities wrote about them. There were producers and preservers, creators and conservers, and the two never met in the middle. The impetus for that to change has, of course, come from artists themselves in large part. From conversations across the last decade, artists working in new ways – using video, photography, digital-born media, and other reproducible media as the tools of their trade – have wondered with myself and with colleagues including Beryl Graham, about how their works will be preserved and known about in the future. Who will look after them? Who will tell their history? Will collections of work by living artists in England only be based in London in future? Or can the regions lead a way forward?

The answer is simple, and indeed obvious, but it has taken Sunderland to act upon a simple idea. We and our colleagues across the north who bring new work into being will ensure it survives, and we will do so by working together – across galleries, universities, and commissioning agencies. Until recently, most of the artworks commissioned at public expense never went into public hands. They were mostly only seen for six or eight weeks, after which they would either be sold to private collectors and investors, or remain in storage. When NGCA and Chisenhale Gallery commissioned what is still Sam Taylor-Wood's largest work to date, Pent Up, back in 1996, my predecessors were not to imagine that not a single edition would end up in public hands; that private collectors would benefit from public largesse; that anyone purchasing the work that public funds paid for would become worth hundreds of thousands of pounds. In the twenty-first century, the relationships between the public and the private sectors needs to change, and in Sunderland it has begun. As austerity bites, and bites hardest of all in the cities of the north of England, it is only going to be through new, imaginative partnership and new ways of thinking that a quiet revolution is going to be brought about. From 2015 NGCA has been working to build a wholly new partnership across the entirety of the north, to ensure that there is a history to tell of twenty-first century art. This is a partnership with some fifteen organisations of international reputation, small and large, including SITE, Drop City, AV Festival, Berwick Film Festival, Tyneside Cinema, Stills, Street Level Photography, Arts & Heritage, Impressions, HOME, and others, as well as CIRCA, and the North East Photography Network closer to our home. It is akin to the partnership between 23 organisations in France under the regional foundation for contemporary art network (FRAC).

It is similar to the network of museums around the Ruhr in Germany who collaborate region wide. But nothing equivalent has existed in England – until now. As of 2016, civic museums' funding is under threat in all our medium and larger cities: acquisition budgets are likely to be cut drastically. Unless action is taken, there will be no 'history' of the art of our lifetimes anywhere outside of London– even despite the heroic support of such organisations such as the Art Fund and Contemporary Art Society.

In the digital age, the idea of a 'museum without walls' makes sense for the first time – just as Beryl Graham had prophesised. Artworks today take an astonishing variety of forms, and a museum of the future needs to reflect that, by

collecting digital artworks just as much, if not more, than tangible ones. We cannot predict the future of art, but we can create a means to ensure that our great cities in the north have access to the finest works of art being made around the world. We have it in our power to do so for everyone, forever, and for free. This, perhaps, is the greatest challenge facing every visual arts institution. In this country, thinking leading the way is again coming out of Sunderland. Starting from a close collaboration between NGCA and National Glass Centre at the University of Sunderland, we have both begun building a museum condition of national importance for our future. It is a collection of artworks that can travel in time, but which can also travel the world. On its travels, it will

The Visual Arts In Sunderland

"In the digital age, the idea of a 'museum without walls' makes sense for the first time - just as Beryl Graham had prophesised."

reveal the breadth and depth of talent that is resident in the north of England, and also the international talent that has worked here under our auspices. The 'local' and the 'international' are not hierarchical terms, in Sunderland: they are of equal importance.

It is no accident that the former Chairman of Arts Council England, Sir Peter Bazalgette, recently called Sunderland the "poster child" for arts-led regeneration in England. It is only where creative individuals have the energy and space to take risks, artistically, that such activities can happen.

Alistair Robinson

Sunderland's Artists

In this section are highlighted three artists from different eras but all of whom have strong Sunderland connections:one was born here; one chose to make it his second home so that he could paint its river and coast; and one who has chronicled the changing city for the last three decades.

Clarkson Stanfield

Clarkson Stanfield was Sunderland's most famous artist. He was born on December 3rd 1793 in a house above a shop in the Playhouse Lane (now Drury Lane) area of Sunderland, close to where it joined Sunderland's High Street.

He was the son of James Stanfield an Irish author, comedian and former seaman. James was a friend of Thomas Clarkson who had campaigned along with William Wilberforce against the slave trade. James named his son Clarkson in honour of the campaigner. Clarkson's mother died when he was only young, and he was raised by his father. As a young man Clarkson moved to South Shields to become a sailor and was forced to join the Royal Navy in 1808. He left the Royal Navy due to ill health in 1814 but he continued to travel the world by sea and made many sketches of his journeys.

He worked as a scene painter for theatres in London, but in 1834 he gave that up to concentrate on his own art, particularly paintings of the sea. Many people loved his work, including King William IV. Stanfield's paintings included naval battle scenes or paintings of places near the sea like of Venice, Antwerp, St. Michael's Mount in Cornwall and Portsmouth harbour. Stanfield was recognised as one of the greatest seascape painters of his time and some of his paintings are still part of the Royal collection. One of his most famous paintings, The Castle of Ischia, is on display at Sunderland Museum and Winter Gardens.

Richard Callaghan

L.S. Lowry

Sunderland has long been home to creative and artistic people, but one of the city's most cherished artistic links is not with a native son or daughter, but rather with famous Mancunian artist L.S. Lowry. Lowry, born in Stretford, Lancashire in 1887, was famous for his paintings of industrial life in the North West.

Lowry's style, including his signature "matchstick men" made him one of the most iconic British artists of the twentieth century. During his lifetime, L.S. Lowry was offered, and rejected, five honours including a knighthood in 1968,

giving him the record for the most rejected British honours.

During his later life, Lowry regularly took holidays at the Seaburn Hotel in Sunderland, taking the time out to draw and paint scenes of the beaches as well as the nearby ports and coal mines. One of Lowry's sketches, on the back of a serviette, can still be seen at the hotel. Lowry discovered Sunderland in 1960 during a chance visit, and the town was to become a second home for him. It provided a retreat from the pressures of city life and also gave him new inspiration. As he said,

'One day I was travelling south from Tyneside and I realised that this was what I had always been looking.

Always staying in the same room at the Seaburn Hotel on the sea front he could look directly out over the North Sea and the shipping which passed by on its way to and from the Wear and Tyne. He became a familiar figure taking regular walks along the promenade and drew and painted many works of the views.

Robert Soden

An established landscape painter, Robert Soden's interest in architecture and urban life began when he lived and worked in Rome in the early 1980s. He has spent much of the last twenty five years recording the changes to the City of Sunderland as it has undergone substantial redevelopment. He sees his work as a continuation of the topographical tradition of Girtin, Cotman and Turner. Soden focuses on the human element of architecture, describing where and how people carry out their lives, in prominent sites as well as less well-documented areas. Soden often uses weather and light as metaphors for the politics of change. The paintings are all made outside in front of the motif and as a result have the veracity of the lived experience.

Robert trained as a painter at Birmingham Polytechnic, 1975-8 and the Royal College of Art, London, 1979-1982. He spent some time painting in Rome where his interest in the city as subject began, he also started to work directly from the subject using water-based materials on paper, a working practice that he continues to this day. He has shown his work in numerous solo and group exhibitions since he graduated most recently at PaintingSunderland, Sunderland the Bluecoat Gallery, Liverpool. He has spent 25 years painting the post-industrial changes to the City of Sunderland. He has undertaken numerous commissions, most recently for the MAC Trust, Sunderland. He is particularly interested in painting major engineering infrastructure projects and is currently recording the construction of the New Wear Crossing.

Richard Callaghan

Photography in the City

WORDS BY *Carol McKay and Amanda Ritson*

NEPN (North East
Photography Network)

Photography In The City

"It proposed that photography, perhaps more than many other art forms, has a 'civic' or public presence "

Hosted and supported by the University of Sunderland and with project funding from Arts Council England through Grants for the Arts, the North East Photography Network (NEPN) is a professional development and commissioning agency for photography, working with international and regional partners to develop a lively and informed context for photographic activity. This chapter reflects on some of its photographic highlights.

Modern cities are dominated by visual images: they surround us on billboards, on moving screens, shop-fronts and numerous other public contexts. Whether we pay them much notice while going about our busy daily lives is another matter, but advertisers (and politicians) certainly think they are important, spending enormous amounts on advertising space so as to constantly reinvent and animate the urban environment. Civic: the first international festival of billboard art (autumn 2011) was an important exploration of this particular kind of commercial space. Organized by

NEPN and the Northern Centre of Photography's Professor John Kippin, Civic was presented across three galleries and thirteen commercial billboards on St Mary's Way and Livingstone Road in Sunderland's City Centre. With exhibitions in the NGCA Project Space, the University's Reg Vardy Gallery and The Place on Athenaeum Street as well as on the street, Civic was true to its name. It proposed that photography, perhaps more than many other art forms, has a 'civic' or public presence and that photographers, like all citizens, are active participants in the lives of their communities. The photographs they make and the contexts in which they are exhibited can help engage others in dialogue, conversation and debate. When displayed in public or commercial contexts, audiences may encounter such photography accidently on the course of their daily lives: the hope is that during the daily commute or shopping trip, some of the photographs may just give people pause for reflection, humorous or provocative: sometimes all at once.

Carol McKay and Amanda Ritson

Photography in the City

The ideas behind Civic emerged out of an innovative photography exchange project developed over the previous two years with colleagues and students at the Folkwang University of the Arts in Essen, Germany. The international connection isn't accidental, as Sunderland and Essen have been twinned cities since 1949. Although Essen is significantly larger, the cities have much in common. Historically, both were engines of their regional and national economies. The physical and social fabric of both cities was immensely damaged during World War Two while, more recently, the experiences of post-industrialization have necessitated reinvention and transformation.

Essen has long been known as a centre for European photography and many well-known photographers have their roots there. The city is also home to the first public collection of modern and contemporary art in Germany (Museum Folkwang) and the photography collections there are internationally renowned. The German term 'Folkwang' implies open access to everyone and it is no accident that both the Museum and the University have this in their title. In 2010, Essen was European Capital of Culture. A festival of photography on billboards, Augen-Blicke became part of the celebrations, with sites all over the city. Involving students and staff from both cities, the festival built on an exciting programme of travel and exchange visits. A group of students from Germany first came to Sunderland in 2009 to experience the culture of the city, to make contacts with other students and photographers in the region and to make new photographic artwork in the process. The exchange was reciprocated the following year, with staff and students from Sunderland travelling to Essen and being hosted by their friends and colleagues there.

Such international partnerships have been an important aspect of Sunderland's photographic activity for more than a decade. In the period 2002-2009, the city became the centre

Photography in the City

of an international network of photographic practitioners, galleries, development agencies and Universities, comprising over thirty-four member organisations and operating in twenty-two countries in Europe and beyond. In the course of this European-funded project that explored the changing face of industry across the globe, more than forty different photographic projects were commissioned, building up an archive and photographic collection held by the University and coordinated by NEPN.

The relationships created during this time have had a real impact on the ability of photographers in the region to produce new projects in an international context. In developing such long-lasting connections with internationally respected centres of photography, Sunderland itself has been widely recognised as such a centre. For NEPN, the exposure to international models of exhibition and experiencing the integration of photographic work into the fabric of cities such as Reggio Emilia, Jyväskylä, Essen, Groningen and others, provided the level of ambition and aspiration necessary for its next major project, The Social.

and experimentation and in turn creating an internationally significant platform for regionally based photographers to showcase their work. To make this happen, NEPN developed important new cultural and commercial partnerships in Sunderland, across the region, nationally and internationally. The Social also developed new community contexts for photographic activity. Photographers created interventions and residencies in social clubs, youth clubs, coffee shops, bars, charity and voluntary organisations and the inclusion of artist-led initiatives and DIY outfits reflected the diversity and ecology of creative practice in the city.

Sunderland was positioned as the nexus of The Social with satellite exhibitions and events across the region, from Durham, through Newcastle and north to Ashington. The Sunderland focus was also important in the commissioning of new projects to be premiered at the festival. Sites of urban regeneration and the repurposing of the landscape were explored by Simon Roberts in the major commission titled The Social: Landscapes of Leisure. Based in Brighton and with an international profile of

"The relationships created during this time have had a real impact on the ability of photographers in the region to produce new projects"

The Social: Encountering Photography was a month-long international celebration of photography across the North East of England. With Sunderland as its hub, The Social ran from 18 October – 16 November 2013. In addition to major gallery and museum exhibitions, the festival incorporated various public contexts and sites and was designed to enable different forms of social engagement with photographic artworks, both indoors and outdoors. Large-scale photographic installations were encountered on shop windows, on the façades of buildings and on a number of advertising sites around the city centre. Tyne & Wear Metro stations were incorporated into the festival, becoming unexpected sites for artworks, intriguing commuters and shoppers and in turn creating a photographic trail that led back into the city. In this way, 'traditional' gallery and museum venues extended their reach to the streets, inviting the public to engage with compelling work both inside and outside of their spaces.

At the heart of The Social was the desire to bring together photographers and artists from around the world, generating a dynamic exchange of photographic practices

exhibition and publication, Roberts developed a new series of photographs that extended his interest in the English social landscape. Rather like classical tableau paintings, his large-scale images reveal Sunderland at leisure: people enjoying (rather uncharacteristically!) sunny days atop Tunstall Hill overlooking the City; preparing a barbecue whilst watching the airshow next to Sunderland Port (itself newly animated and redeveloping); surveying the former site of Herrington pit from the grand neo-classical folly Penshaw Monument or kicking a football against the backdrop of Lakeside Village high rise flats. The images were shown in a range of indoor and outdoor contexts, mirroring the festival's indoor/outdoor theme and infiltration of varied social contexts.

Sunderland's old Fire Station was the site for one of The Social's major new commissions by north-east based photographer Juliet Chenery-Robson. This iconic building on an historically important thorough-fare was still something of a dormant giant in 2013 and the temporary photographic installation on its façade became synonymous with the aims of The Social. Juliet's series of large-scale portraits were a development of an on-going photographic exploration of the

effects on individuals of the much-misunderstood illness ME. The portraits of ME sufferers with their eyes closed offered a metaphorical representation of their invisible illness and lives lived in the shadow of alienation, social exclusion, controversy and loss of identity. The sitters are presented here as coolly formal but highly individualized portraits. As Juliet has said, by closing their eyes, the sitters in her portraits invite the viewer to open theirs.

Other projects had a participatory element to help create a contemporary spectacle of photography in the city centre. Dow Wasiksiri, a leading Thai photographer, was invited to Sunderland as part of the UK premiere of The (Post) colonial Photo Studio, an exhibition at Northern Gallery for Contemporary Art which explored traditions of portraiture and commercial studios in former western colonies. During his visit, Dow also created a roving, pop-up studio and invited Sunderland residents to pose against fabrics and giant backdrops that were specially reprinted from historic photographs. Sourced from the city's museum and local

studies collections, these archive portraits were made in some of the many Victorian and Edwardian photo-studios that once thrived in the city. Out of the archives, here they were again, former Sunderland residents and visitors posing with their descendants.

This kind of playful intervention in the social space was revisited in 2015 when north-east based artist Kuba Ryniewicz was commissioned to develop a Fantasy Photo-Studio, a city centre pop-up for the Sunderland2021 launch weekend. The vision was to create a humorous and engaging play on the aspirations of the city to develop as a cultural destination, borrowing references from traditions of the holiday snapshot and tourist information brochures. Like a fashion director, Kuba invited visitors to have their portraits taken, instructing them to adopt various mysterious postures and gestures and photographing them against a blank white backdrop. Studio assistants dropped these portraits into colourful digital backdrops, instantly transporting people to fantasy worlds conjured up from Sunderland landmarks and

Photography in the City

in return giving back a humorous photographic souvenir to be taken away.

For the same launch weekend, NEPN also revisited the Fire Station façade on High Street West. Julian Germain, internationally recognized photographic artist and Visiting Professor of the Northern Centre of Photography, was invited to make portraits of babies born on Wearside that summer. The babies were photographed within the first two weeks of life in their own homes and the commission was intended to provide a metaphor for the transformation or rebirth of the site and the city centre as a whole, whilst also celebrating a new generation of Sunderland residents. The large-scale photographs, simply titled Newborns, not only ask us to consider the mystery of being human, but also the mystery of the future, what will it hold for them? Julian reflects on the intrigue of the photographs: 'how can we possibly imagine what they are imagining? How will they turn out? What does the future hold for them? As adults, we are also presented with a serious challenge, because we are responsible for the world they will grow up in.'

In these ways, NEPN continues to support work that challenges, questions and engages. Berlin-based photographer Mark Curran was recently commissioned to develop a new strand in his long-term project investigating the hidden forces of the global financial market. The Economy of Appearances premiered at the Noorderlicht Photofestival in the Netherlands in 2015, before travelling to New York Photoville, from where it will return to Sunderland for its UK premier. These are the international contexts in which NEPN continues to develop new photographic commissions and opportunities for artists, with a view to presenting these alongside others developed by its regional and national partners. The next iteration of The Social, planned for 2021, will provide just such a platform. Once again, the city itself will become a site for photographic intervention, exchange and engagement, running alongside major gallery and museum exhibitions. And in this way, Sunderland will again produce and host some of the best in contemporary photography.

Sunderland Shorts Film Festival

Sunderland Shorts is an annual, three-day film festival that showcases short films from all over the world. The aim of the festival is to celebrate the art of filmmaking and to showcase the best short films from across the world in Sunderland. It is a festival that enhances the knowledge and skills of emerging filmmakers through networking and development opportunities with experienced sector professionals. It will soon become a major contributor to the cultural calendar of Sunderland and the rest of the region.

All films featured in the festival are under 20 minutes in length and are shown at pop-up cinemas in venues around Sunderland. Each screening is around 90 minutes, and contains a mix of genres, themes and styles so there is something for every audience member to tap into. There are highs and lows, laughter and sadness, reflection and relaxation over the course of every 90 minutes.

Believe it or not, the festival all started with George Washington. Sunderland has a unique, historic relationship with Washington DC, through the link of first USA President George Washington to his ancestral home at the 13th century Washington Old Hall in Washington Village, Tyne and Wear.

In 2006, because of this link, Sunderland became the only non-capital city to sign a Friendship Agreement with Washington DC, fostering and developing economic, educational and cultural relationships between the two cities, for example, Sunderland now enjoys a strong American presence, creating thousands of jobs particularly in the city's Advanced Manufacturing and Automotive sectors. There has also been a lot of Creative Industry collaborations between Washington DC and Sunderland glass and ceramics artists including joint exhibitions, residencies and workshop exchanges.

Sunderland Shorts Film Festival was also born out of this partnership. It was established in 2014 and was conceived and developed in collaboration with DC Shorts, a film festival based in Washington DC with a fourteen year history, which has gone from strength to strength and is now one of the most respected film festivals in the USA and internationally.

Since then, Sunderland Shorts has grown bigger and better as each year goes by. It is very much a collaboratively run festival. It is led by the International and Creative Industries teams at Sunderland City Council and delivered in partnership between various local businesses such as Bureau Design Ltd, the Music, Arts and Culture Trust, Northern Bear Films, Creo Communications and M.A.D. Communications. Supporters and sponsors include Sunderland Business Group, Sunderland BID, See it Do it, The Bridges, Printing Services, Northern Productions Ltd, Siglion and Independent. Then there is also a hard-working army of volunteer reviewers and festival helpers.

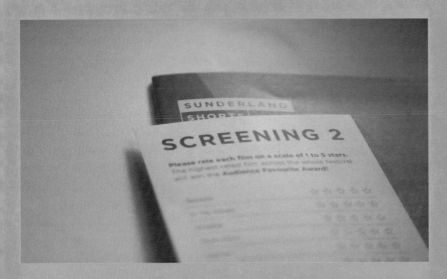

WORDS BY *Helen Green*
Director, The Fire Station

Rollercoaster Sunderland!

A personal view of performing arts in the city

"Life in Sunderland at the moment is a bit like being on a roller coaster ride"

Life in Sunderland at the moment is a bit like being on a roller coaster ride – whether you support the Black Cats or work in the cultural sector! I'm not a Mackem – not even from the north east, but after 25 years working in and observing the cultural life of a number of cities around the UK, it's the bumpiest ride I've ever had... but the thrills are becoming more significant and the dips less stomach churning. When I arrived in Sunderland in 2008, I have to confess I was a bit bewildered by a city that, at that point, didn't utilise culture and its positive effects, whether they be social, educative or economic, to the extent that other cities I had lived in did. Those that worked in the city's cultural sector were powerless to bring real influence without the strong, passionate cultural leadership so vital to any city. It very quickly became apparent that whilst Sunderland has a handful of iconic cultural buildings – The Empire Theatre, Sunderland Museum and Winter Gardens, National Glass Centre, that contain and reflect Sunderland's soul and identity, it has far

less than its fair share of cultural provision. Scratch beneath the surface and you would find yourself uncovering small pockets of professional artists beavering away against the odds trying their best to make a living, and community arts groups achieving fantastic results in their own quiet way.

Take performing arts, my particular area, and you will find in the city at present: a large scale commercial theatre, a small scale studio theatre and a handful of professional performance companies (theatre and dance) alongside a wealth of amateur dramatic societies, youth theatres and dance groups. So, whilst the amateur sector flourishes, professional, contemporary performing arts has a low profile, which, for one of the largest cities in the north east, should not be the case. Is it surprising that audiences for the performing arts in Sunderland are low? The Cultural Spring is doing sterling work to address this lack of engagement but its wider remit covers all art forms which is why I feel compelled to champion the cause of performing arts. I feel

there needs to be a greater variety of theatre, dance and spoken word on offer to audiences and more opportunities for artists to perform in the city – whether they are from down the road or from another continent.

Ask any Sunderland resident to name a theatre in Sunderland and they will immediately offer The Empire Theatre, a grand Edwardian theatre opened in 1907 by the vaudeville star Vesta Tilley. It has a rich history as a variety theatre, hosting the likes of Tommy Steele, The Beatles, Helen Mirren and Sid James (who notoriously haunts his old dressing room after suffering a fatal heart attack on stage). It boasts the largest stage between London and Edinburgh and has seating for over 1800 and a total capacity of 2,200. Once famous for its variety programme it now presents large scale musicals, opera and ballet, and frequently hosts tours that have emerged from London's West End, recent notable productions being War Horse and Billy Elliott. The Empire also runs a thriving creative learning programme that is able

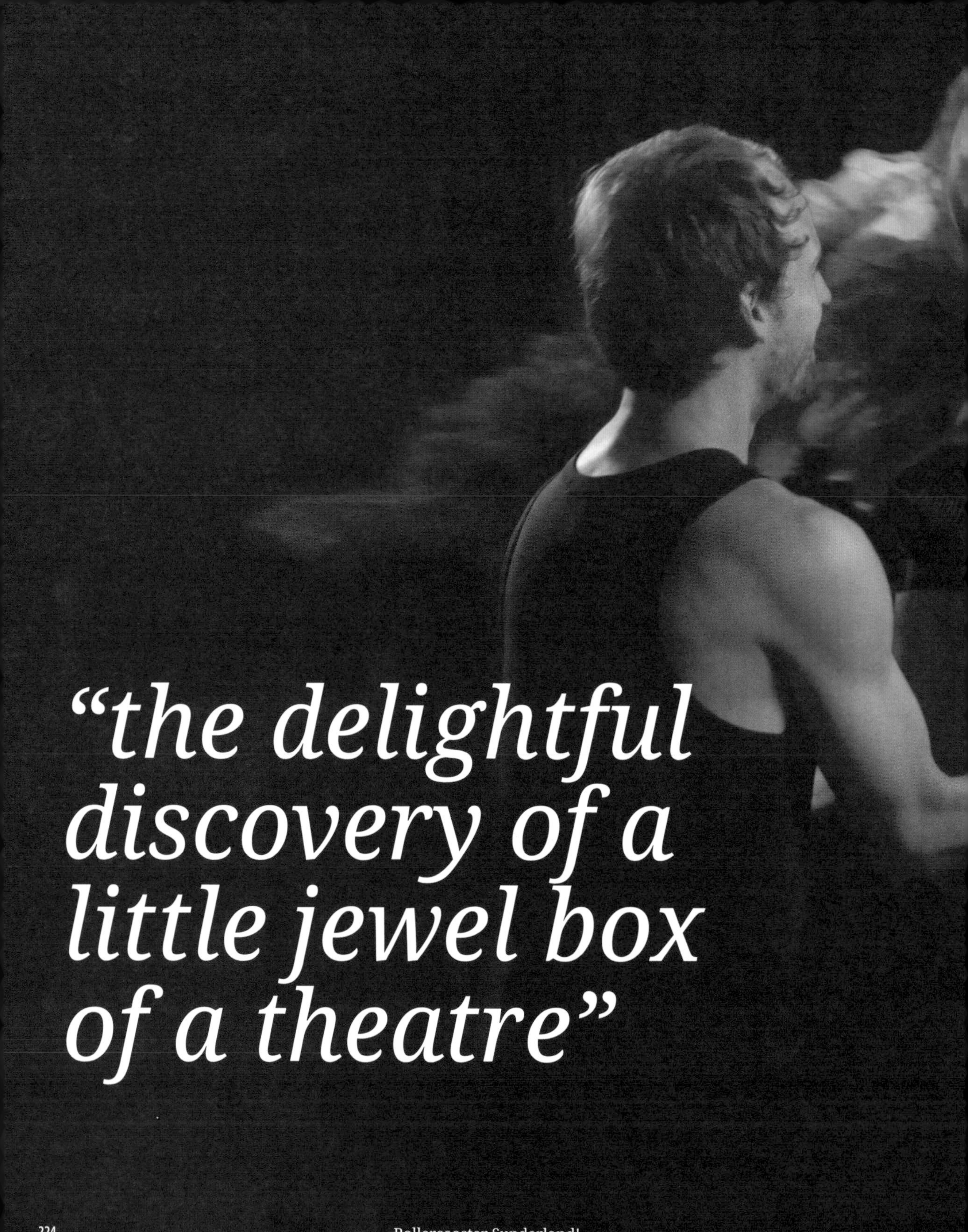

"*the delightful
discovery of a
little jewel box
of a theatre*"

to link community based projects to shows on its stage, such as the recent Get Curious project, linked to the National Theatre tour of The Curious Incident of the Dog in the Night-time, where it joined forces with other cultural organisations to provide opportunities for children and young people with autistic spectrum disorder. The people of Sunderland are rightly proud of its flagship venue that pulls in audiences from all over the north of England, many in large groups, who spill out of their coaches at the theatre entrance and pile back on the waiting vehicles at the end of the show – if only these visits could be extended by an hour or two, the impact on the city centre would be hugely beneficial, for local businesses and city centre vibrancy!

The Empire Theatre is a vital component of the city's cultural life, but what a city like Sunderland needs is not just the big, popular, wow factor shows it presents. It needs to have a wider range of choice and affordability in different scale venues that can support performing arts in other ways. Venues that can present new writing, original, innovative and edgy performance, local and regional mid- career or emerging artists, performances for children and families, performances that support the school curriculum, venues that can host school and community productions or ones that provide intimacy for spoken word and solo artists. There are many fabulous productions touring the country that never get to Sunderland because there are no suitable venues. Well that was the case, but things have been steadily improving in recent years and are about to get even better!

In 2008 I was looking for a change and a new challenge, and boy did I get one! Having moved from managing a national and international touring theatre company, I took on the newly created post of Creative Director at Arts Centre Washington (ACW). Located to the west of the main city, a multi purpose arts centre converted from a derelict 19th century farm that was redeveloped to provide a cultural centre for the residents of the 1960's utopian "new town" vision of Washington. What I discovered on arrival was a venue in the doldrums.

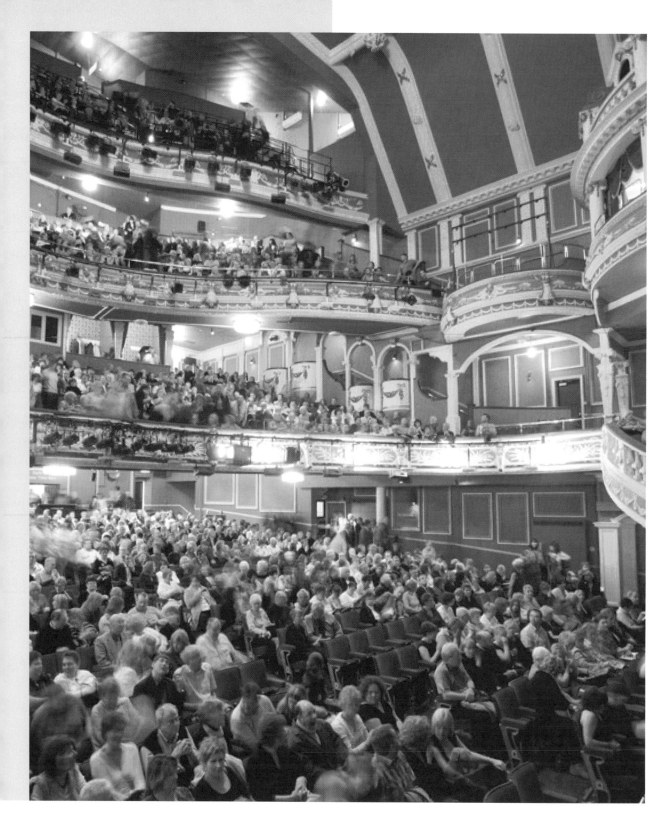

226 Rollercoaster Sunderland!

However, the delightful discovery of a little jewel box of a theatre converted from the old stone barn, both intimate and atmospheric and, at that point, totally unused made it all worthwhile. Early funding from the Northern Rock Foundation helped kick-start the theatre programme and subsequent inclusion in a number of groups, networks and strategic initiatives such as the North East Children's Theatre Consortium, Venues North and the North East Artists Development group have all helped put ACW back on the map. A theatre programmer has to balance a number of factors: personal taste, quality of product, and what will appeal to audiences. However, I soon realised my programming experience had been built up in much larger cities like Edinburgh, Manchester and London, where there is the critical mass of confident theatregoers to ensure audiences for the more original work favoured by contemporary theatre artists. So it was a slow, uphill climb persuading local residents to sample theatre or dance that is very different from the entertainment on offer at other local venues. I constantly search for work that will be particularly

"theatre must entertain but also be able to reflect our society, be provocative and emotional"

relevant and more attractive to local residents whilst trying not to compromise my belief that theatre must entertain but also be able to reflect our society, be provocative and emotional – appeal to our minds as well as our hearts. ACW has established a reputation along these lines for high quality, original and occasionally quirky performance and has developed a niche for itself in the regional arts ecology.

In Sunderland it inhabits the opposite end of the spectrum to The Empire Theatre In terms of scale, funding and programme; and at present is the only other fully professional theatre in the city. Whilst ACW is continually attracting new visitors from Washington, Newcastle, Gateshead, and County Durham, audiences from Sunderland struggle to overcome the barrier of the A19 that slices between Sunderland and Washington alienating the residents of the main city from its only other professional performance venue! The arts centre's inability to overcome this physical and psychological barrier for Sunderland audiences to visit our fabulous theatre perplexed me! I finally came to the realisation that if Mohammed wouldn't come to the mountain... resulting

in a programme called Sunderland Stages, funded by Arts Council England. The much anticipated new venue for Sunderland, The Fire Station, that will at last provide that much needed mid-scale space that originally grew out of the call for a music venue of this size but will also include theatre, dance and spoken word in its programme. It will sit next to The Empire Theatre providing a complementary programme and both venues will form the core of a new cultural quarter for the city. The city's original, derelict fire station will be re- invented to house a restaurant and bar on the ground floor and dance and drama studios on the first floor. Both Dance City and Live Theatre are involved in the remit of these studios bringing their knowledge, skills and experience to ensure the highest quality learning and participation programmes get off to a good start. A new 450 seat auditorium will be located to the side and accessed via The Fire Station. This new venue will be able to serve all those gaps left blank by The Empire and ACW. It will be able to programme regional, national and international artists who are at the top of their game, whose practice fits better

at the mid-scale. It is also perfectly placed to nurture and support student, postgraduate and emerging artists, providing resources and expertise in a very central location. It will help re-animate the city centre Keel Square area and the massive new developments happening on the Vaux site and, fingers crossed, play a key role in Sunderland's bid to become City of Culture in 2021.

There are other performance spaces across the city. By way of contrast, close by is the Royalty Theatre, a community theatre owned and managed by its volunteers who contribute to the theatre's upkeep through subscription based membership. Sitting on the edge of the city centre, this venue is also a traditional proscenium arch design, yet small scale with another smaller studio space. It appeals to a home audience with a programme of traditional, tried and tested theatre. A recent addition to the city is Sunderland College's brand, spanking new theatre which inhabits its new Visual and Performing Arts building at its Bede campus. This space is primarily for the use of students but does also host professional touring companies. There are also a number of smaller, non theatre venues such as Pop Recs and Independent whose main focus is on music. However, they have occasionally presented small scale theatre and regular spoken word events. The Holy Trinity Church in the east end of the city is, with support from the Heritage Lottery Fund, developing itself as The Canny Space, a heritage and arts venue.

Whilst things are looking up on the venue side, life as a Sunderland theatre or dance company, or spoken word artist has been more of a struggle. At the time of writing there is one fully professional theatre company that employs permanent staff operating from its own base in the city, and a handful of theatre and dance companies that present work

Helen Green

professionally on an occasional, ad hoc basis subject to funding availability. None of these companies are recipients, of Arts Council England National Portfolio funding. Performances more often operate on a profit share amongst the performers and production team. These few companies must be acknowledged for their staying power, when most in their position prefer to work where there are more accessible resources, developmental support and performance opportunities. The few that have stayed do so as they have been able to find a niche offer that ensures their sustainability delivering workshops and performances for corporate events, staff training and so on – often at the expense of their own practise or fundability. The tide is slowly turning as artists are able to articulate their practice and become more adept at meeting funding requirements. The cultural sector is starting to help itself through the *What's Next* forum, disseminating information on funding, marketing and producing advice. I am also involved in a group of Sunderland arts organisations that offer support and development to emerging artists in the city. The new dance and drama studios at The Fire Station supported by Dance City and Live Theatre will be a real boost to local performing artists. Who knows, maybe a home grown professional theatre or dance company may be performing on the stage of the new venue by the time we get to 2021? Interestingly, the amateur sector is flourishing

in the city. I have already mentioned The Royalty Theatre whose members manage the venue and produce and perform in up to seven productions a year. Even older is Sunderland Theatre Company which can trace its history back to 1893. Its focus has mainly been on traditional musicals performed in a variety of venues. Arts Centre Washington is home to Washington Theatre Group who produce approximately three productions each year including its enormously popular pantomime. There are many more such groups all over the city, alongside the more commercially operated theatre and dance schools, all with healthy memberships. There is a huge well of enthusiasm for theatre amongst the members of these amateur organisations and the audiences for the plays they present. Whilst Sunderland Stages includes The Royalty as one of its host venues, more cross-over and collaborative initiatives with the amateur sector are required to encourage audiences to sample more contemporary professional theatre and develop confidence in seeing innovative work that is often immersive or interactive.

The education sector plays a vital role in nurturing talent and creating confident cultural consumers of the future. Sunderland University and Sunderland College inhabit important and influential roles in the support and development of performing arts in the city. Both have high quality, active performing arts departments who are increasingly

Helen Green

engaging with the professional sector in the drive to develop more indigenous performing artists who move and work in their home city rather than float off to where the work can be found within the region or the UK. Sunderland University's Drama department takes over ACW each May to present Sunfest, where each of the three undergraduate years present approximately eight plays between them. They are also a core partner in Sunderland Stages with ACW and MAC Trust, as is Sunderland College and both will host productions brought into the city as part of this programme over the next 18 months. The college's new venue is a fantastic resource for its students and also enables it to programme occasional professional companies, some of which take up residencies in the college to work on a more regular basis with the students, such as Fertile Ground Dance Company. Enthusiasm for performing arts in the primary and secondary sector is less easy to define, especially when most of the Learning and Education specialists attached to cultural establishments lean more towards visual arts and crafts. Some schools are incredibly passionate about the arts and have very knowledgeable, skilled and dedicated drama and dance teachers, but there is still a huge unexplored mutually beneficial relationship between the city's schools and its cultural venues. For example, ACW has a fabulous relationship with one local academy; works with many of its teachers on projects, welcomes its pupils to its productions and delivers performing arts workshops in school. Other local secondary schools are less aware of the work done by Sunderland cultural venues. This lack of interaction isn't helped by the government's erosion of arts and creativity subjects in school in favour of the STEM subjects. It is so vital that the cultural sector guarantees provision for children and young people to discover and develop their love of any art form, not just the performing arts. On the one hand we can help support those committed teachers delivering after school drama and dance clubs but we must also fight to retain the rich and varied programme of participatory activities delivered for children and young people by our cultural organisations in Sunderland. We must ensure the stability and continuation of such groups as the Empire Youth Theatre, The Royalty Theatre Youth Programme, Washington Senior Youth Theatre, Washington Junior Youth Theatre, Rainbow Youth Theatre, Dance Jam, Pallion Youth Action, Bounce and Boom and many more. Not just for the myriad life skills they endow but because as the future of the city, we want them to stay and thrive as artists, as cultural leaders, as confident consumers of culture and well rounded citizens in the new, vibrant city we are working hard to develop. Sunderland Cultural Partnership's Learning Group is working hard to fly

"high quality, active performing arts departments who are increasingly engaging with the professional sector in the drive to develop more indigenous performing artists who move and work in their home city"

the flag for creativity in schools and raise the profile of the city's cultural establishments with teachers, promoting Sunderland as the first Arts Award city in the UK. Life is very different these days. There is optimism. Whilst local authority cuts loom, culture is now viewed by the city leaders as playing a crucial role in its regeneration. The creation of Sunderland Culture brings strong, visionary cultural leadership working with a band of experienced arts managers to drive the vision forward. Performing artists are becoming more confident with their ideas and making more work. More and more really interesting and original performance is being presented in the city: Miracle - An Opera for Sunderland written by David Almond premiered at Sunderland Minster, subsequently winning a Journal Culture Award whilst Sunderland Museum and Winter Gardens hosted Lemn Sissay performing his poetry in tandem with their Picture the Poet exhibition. Cultural Spring's commissions have

"An honorary Mackem - I hope?"

resulted in Invisible Flock's Bring the Happy and Wildworks' A Great Night Out, both of which delved into local lives for inspiration. Arts Centre Washington has found real success with its children's theatre programme, whilst Sunderland Stages continues its programme of touring performance which may lead to further opportunities in the future as a commissioner and producer of new performance work. At last there will be a new venue, The Fire Station, providing artists with opportunities to stay - research, develop, collaborate, rehearse and perform in their home city. Sunderland audiences will have somewhere new to visit; to be entertained, moved, enthused and inspired. And to top it all the city will do its very best to become City of Culture in 2021. Sunderland's cultural life won't be a rollercoaster ride any more – I wish I could say the same about the football team! An honorary Mackem – I hope?

Sunderland Stages

Sunderland Stages presents live performance in hidden, unexpected and favourite venues across the city. Funded by Arts Council England, the programme aims to engage Sunderland residents in the performing arts by presenting the highest quality theatre, dance and spoken word that is relevant, accessible and entertaining. Many of Sunderland's cultural buildings such as Sunderland Museum and Winter Gardens, Pop Recs, The Royalty Theatre, the Independent music venue and The Canny Space have hosted performances. Other sites, unused to catering for performance, are adapted for the needs of the programme such as Sunderland Minster, Central Library, The Funky Indian Restaurant, St Mary's car park and Roker seafront promenade. Others have been chosen to attract a particular audience such as Weekend Rockstars performed at the Students Union; Not Quite a Pub Quiz at The Dun Cow pub or others where the obvious links are too good to be true, as with Lands of Glass including a glass orchestra... where else could it perform but at the National Glass Centre!

The Sunderland Stages programme has been able to attract a host of artists and companies who otherwise would happily motor on up the A1 destined for all points north oblivious to a whole city of potential new audiences. The programme has included performances specially designed for children such as Horse & Bamboo's Hansel and Gretel; or Zest Theatre's Thrive for young people, or the more traditional themes of wartime in Swan Canaries or Red Ladder's Were Not Going Back about the miners' strike, to play to older audiences.

The programme also aims to include artists at different stages of their career from the well-established artists and companies such as Third Angel, Ballet Lorent, Paines Plough, Ridiculusmus, Kate Fox and Luke Wright to newcomers such as Middle Child, Rash Dash, Curious Monkey and Rowan McCabe.

Helen Green

THE·LAMBTON·WORM

Wearside 'Folk' and Tradition

Wearside 'Folk' and Tradition

"Fascinating story and legend of the Lambton Worm"

The North East of England in general has a well-founded reputation for its folk/music hall songs and tales and Wearside has a role to play alongside rural Northumberland and Tyneside in forging that reputation. The often-used term 'Wearside' is an interesting one as it embraces not only the former town, port and borough of Sunderland but also significant centres of population to the west. Among these centres are the former coal-mining communities of Hetton le Hole, Houghton le Spring as well as the various villages old and new that came together in the mid twentieth century to form the 'new town' of Washington. Significantly, many of these Wearside traditions survive as living ones and still have a role to play in the city's cultural life.

The survival of tradition can be seen with reference to three tales told beautifully in a 1940s publication entitled 'Folk Tales of the North Country'. (This book, aimed at youngsters, was published in the 'Teaching of English' series).

Within Sunderland's boundaries is the setting for the fascinating story and legend of the Lambton Worm. The story goes that in medieval times, Sir John Lambton, something of a reprobate, spent his Sundays fishing in the River Wear when he should have been at church. While fishing one day he caught a strange looking worm-like creature which he disposed of by throwing into a nearby well. Soon after he was called upon to join the Crusades and while he was away, the worm increased in size and terrorised the neighbourhood. It was noted in particular for its ability to wrap its tail three times around a local hill (still known as Worm Hill and dominating the riverside in the Fatfield area of the city). Many efforts were made to overcome the monster but all failed. Then Lambton returned from his travels a reformed man and began to seek out ways of killing the creature. Eventually he came across a local witch who offered him a special suit of armour on the understanding that he killed

Beda venerabilis

the first living creature he came across after seeing off the worm. Lambton agreed and arranged for an old family hound, not long for this world, to be released into his sight as soon as the worm was dead. The magic armour allowed him to rid the neighbourhood of the 'Lambton Worm' but, in the excitement which followed the knight's father ran out of the house and was the first to come into Lambton's view. Ignoring the witch's instructions, Lambton killed the hound. The result – or so the legend goes – was a curse on the Lambton family namely that none of the heirs should die a timely death and until fairly recently this has proved the case.

In the mid Victorian period a song called 'The Lambton Worm' was composed for a north east pantomime and became so sought after that it was later published in a collection of 'traditional' songs. Over the years it has become more and more popular in and around Sunderland and can now be classed as a Wearside folk song and part of a living tradition. Travel around local primary schools and you will find numerous youngsters able to chant the memorable chorus;

> **Wisht lads, haad yer gobs – I'll tell you all an aaful story**
> **Wisht lads haad yer gobs I'll tell ye boot the worm**

Lewis Carroll's poem, Jabberwocky, is said to be based on the Lambton Worm, a significant illustrated book on the story was recently produced by a local author and schools and other organisations often put together musical and dramatic productions based on the tale.

Nothing perhaps encapsulates the folk tradition of the modern city of Sunderland more than the story of the Dun Cow. Once more 'according to legend', in Saxon times the body of the great St Cuthbert was carried from place to place in the north east as his monastic 'carers' sought a permanent home for it after his death on Holy Island. For a significant period, the body rested at Chester le Street just to the west of Sunderland but had to be moved as Chester came under threat from Norse invaders. After wandering for a while, the monks and the saint's body came to halt at a place called Wrdelau. This is likely to have been an atmospheric Wearside hill or law situated between the town of Sunderland and Houghton le Spring and known today as Warden Law. While stranded here, the monks had a vision which told them to seek out Dunholm as a resting place for the saint. However nobody had heard of Dunholm. The twentieth century author of the folk tales takes up the story:

Keith Gregson

Wearside 'Folk' and Tradition

Just at that moment, two women passed near. One was driving her cattle home to milk, and the other was looking about her anxiously as though she had lost something. Then as they passed, the second called out in a loud voice, "Neighbour, I have lost the red cow with the short horn. Have you seen her?" And the other replied, "Yes, I saw her a few minutes ago. She has strayed to Dunholm."

When the monks heard the word Dunholm they jumped up and ran to the milkmaid.

"Dunholm is the very place for which we are searching," they cried. "Can you show us the way".

The milkmaid duly obliged, the original Durham church/cathedral was set up on a hill protected by a curve in the River Wear and the legend of the Dun Cow was born.

Today the legend is celebrated in Sunderland in the form of the Dun Cow pub, a magnificently restored and double award winning Edwardian real ale venue. It serves as watering hole for the neighbouring Empire Theatre, has a musical staff and a reputation for regular live music. Interestingly too the city seems to have adopted as an anthem an ancient music hall song of the same name. An amusing ditty covering (the probably mythical) attempts by pub regulars to consume the contents of a pub as it burnt down, it became a favourite in the 1970s thanks to the singing of Sunderland born and bred Paddy Hilton, who was the front man for the popular local folk group, Frigate. Recorded by the BBC in a visit to the Belford House folk club in the 1970s, in the early 21st century the song and its recording were picked up by internationally known local indie band the Futureheads as they were putting together an acapella album called 'Rant'. The song with catchy chorus has enjoyed a revival with young and old alike. Ask Wearsiders who 'Brown and the boys' shouted for when 'The Old Dun Cow 'caught fire and many

will tell you (loudly and musically) it was 'MACINTYRE'!

The next tale is one with considerable historical contextuality if little in the way of hard evidence. Bede is a massively important figure in the history of the Western World because of his contribution to literature both religious and historical. It is now acknowledged universally that he was born on Wearside in Saxon times and spent his life in and around the north east. Known world-wide as 'The Venerable Bede', he forms the subject of this tale which purports to tell the story behind his 'title'.

According to legend in old age Bede lost his sight and one day a young boy decided to use the saint's blindness for his own amusement. He told Bede that there was a large audience waiting to hear him speak and pray and led the old man out into a clearing where there was little but stones, grass and bushes and told him to begin his sermon. Bede duly obliged and the youngster sat smiling as the saint addressed nobody but Mother Nature. Suddenly there was a mighty roar as thousands of raised voices chanted the words 'The Venerable Bede'. To his surprise, the boy saw that the voices were coming from the very stones, bushes and grass he had led the saint to believe were his audience. Humbled by his experience, the boy led the man back to his monk's cell and began to repeat the story until it was accepted that Bede was indeed to be 'venerated'.

Today Bede's bones rest alongside those of Cuthbert in Durham Cathedral but his roots in Sunderland and in particular in and around St Peter's Church in Bishopwearmouth are recognised as an important part of Wearside culture. A modern secondary school bears his name and title, countless efforts have been (and are still being) made to raise the profile of the church and its surroundings. As is the case with the Lambton Worm, the work of both

Bede and his mentor (and patron saint of Sunderland) Benedict Biscop often feature in local musical and dramatic productions. A number of schools also sing a modern assembly action song dedicated to the two saints and bearing the title 'Two People, Two Churches, Two Rivers'.

Reference to song brings us neatly to an examination of the role in Wearside culture of what can be regarded as 'traditional' song. Sunderland and some of its musically creative inhabitants had an important role to play in the national folk revival which gathered pace from the 1950s. During this period there were folk clubs at the Londonderry, the Blue Bell, Belford House and the Glebe and a number of these survived well into the 1970s and 1980s. Washington hosts the Davy Lamp Folk Club which has gained a reputation in the folk world as one of the most significant and durable of venues. In 2001, the club was designated BBC Folk Club of the Year.

Despite something of a lean time in the late twentieth century, folk in its wider sense has enjoyed a revival in the city in recent years. A monthly afternoon at the Stumble Inn (formerly 70's folk venue The Glebe) brings together some fifty or sixty enthusiasts – with well over half of them performers. This gathering has become increasingly popular because of its relaxed and enjoyable approach to live entertainment. Performers are even called to order by the ringing of the 'Birtley Bell' – a hand bell formerly used at the now defunct Birtley Folk Club in County Durham. This club had an international reputation as base camp for the 'Elliots of Birtley' – a family known for its mining songs. Members of the family attend the Stumble Inn session on a regular basis. In 2016, one member of the Elliot family enlivened a Stumble Inn session by celebrating 63 years of marriage with a lusty duet with her husband. '

Wearside has also produced its own successful folk singers. Both Bob Fox and Jez Lowe, frequent headliners at large folk festivals, have their roots in Wearside clubs. Bob, who recently

Wearside 'Folk' and Tradition

starred in the West End production of War Horse, was resident at the Davy Lamp in its early days. Jez, nominated for both best folk artist and best contemporary song in 2015, was one of the driving forces behind the 1970s student folk club at Langham Tower. Still active today and a regular at the Stumble Inn is Ed Pickford. From a mining family in the now city suburb of Shiny Row, Ed had composed a number of mining related songs which have come to be regarded as folk songs themselves in traditional circles. Among his songs are Ah Cud Hew, Farewell Johnny Miner and The Workers Song.

The north east of England is one of the regions of the country with a reputation for its older 'traditional songs'. In this respect it bears comparison to both London and Liverpool. Within the region, Wearside has a role to play in this respect not only with recognised anthems already referred to such as 'The Lambton Worm' but also with equally old songs which have been unearthed in recent times. Perhaps the oldest of these dates back to the late eighteenth century/early nineteenth century and the story it tells has some grounding in truth. It relates to the tale of a hermit with the nickname Spottee who lived in a cave in Roker Ravine. Spottee was a strange looking, frightening yet basically harmless character who defended his cave and its surrounds by bawling loudly at intruders. The fishwives of Whitburn (whose cottages are still inhabited today) were so afraid of him that instead of walking along the beach to the Fish Quay close to the river mouth they 'took to a coble (fishing boat) and went by sea.' The Sunderland fishwives were also frightened of this man – who gained his nickname due to the colourful dotted garment he wore. On one occasion, the hermit had set up a fire on the beach and an incoming vessel had mistaken it for the nearby lighthouse. As a result it ended up stranded on the rocks. Although no lives were lost, Spottee was blamed and his fearsome reputation confirmed. The original words and tune are to be found in an early nineteenth century publication. The first verse runs;

Come Sunderland people and listen to me
And a funny old tale I'll tell to ye
About one called Spottee – lived down by the quay
And neither a harbour or house had he

In the early 21st century a chorus with actions was added so the song could be performed by schoolchildren. This goes:

Spottee was here, Spottee was there
Spottee was nearly everywhere
Spottee was scary. Spottee was grand
Spottee the hermit of Sunderland

Keith Gregson

Wearside 'Folk' and Tradition

"In 2009, Sunderland was one of the few urban centres in England to take up a national offer of producing its own Singing History songbook"

The same story formed the subject of a short professional film made by the members of Monkwearmouth School as part of a major cultural project. With the help of nationally respected producers, youngsters parodied the original song with a highly amusing and entertain rap version of Spottee's tale.

In 2009, Sunderland was one of the few urban centres in England to take up a national offer of producing its own Singing History songbook. At the time Sunderland's director of music in schools wrote of this venture:

Sunderland City Council has been working in partnership with Sing London and Tyne and Wear Archives and Museums to produce a songbook about Sunderland that will inspire people of all ages to learn about Sunderland's past through song.

When the collection was published, it contained a number of songs with traditional roots – old penny street ballads such as The Pretty Girls of Sunderland and The Boat Race on the Wear plus music hall songs like The Sunderland Trip and the Lads upon the Wear. There was also a street ballad called The Rigs of Sunderland Fair and since its publication enthusiastic local song collector Eileen Richardson has come up with another contemporary song about the fair. Eileen has also collected ditties relating to other aspects of Sunderland life including a fascinating one about the effect of the coming of the railways on the keelmen who had for years transported coal along the River Wear. Also in the collection is a sea shanty which was noted down from a Sunderland sailor in 1863. Entitled 'The Meeting of the First to take charge of a ship', this is a fascinating and unusual version of 'Blow the Man Down'. It is perhaps unsurprising that songs connected with the sea should end up in Sunderland. In the early days of recording, researcher James Madison Carpenter visited the homes of retired Sunderland mariners in the town's Trafalgar Square and Assembly Garth. Here he gathered and recorded a significant number of sea shanties. These recordings, on wax cylinders, now reside in the archives of Sheffield University and remain a valuable resource. As working songs, sea shanties were rarely repeated in the very same version so those collected in Sunderland are likely to be unique and of continuing interest.

It is clear that Wearside has a significant traditional legacy which survives as part of a living culture. Those currently involved in maintaining this culture – whether it be in pubs, clubs, schools, museums or libraries – sense an ever increasing stirring of interest in this area among Wearsiders. It is an interest which deserves to be explored and extended.

Sunderland's Heritage Buildings

Penshaw Monument

Constructed in 1844, the folly officially known as the Earl of Durham's Monument stands atop the 446-foot Penshaw Hill. Presented by Charles Vane, the 3rd Marquis of Londonderry, Penshaw monument is dedicated to the memory of John Lambton, the 1st Earl of Durham. Lambton, Lord Privy Seal under Prime Minister Charles Grey, was known as "Radical Jack" and helped to draft the 1832 Reform Bill, before becoming the first Governor General of the Province of Canada from 1838 to 1839.

A half-sized replica of the A half-sized replica of the Temple of Hephaestus in Athens, Penshaw Monument's foundation stone was laid on August 28, 1844 by Thomas Dundas, the 2nd Earl of Zetland, four years after John Lambton's death. The Monument remained the property of the Lambton family until 1939 when the 5th Earl of Durham, also called John Lambton, gave the monument to the National Trust. It is often seen by people from Sunderland and Wearside as a symbolic landmark sitting proudly above the city and its surrounding area. In recent years, it has lit with different colours to signify a special event or to show Sunderland's solidarity with people in other countries following a tragedy.

Richard Callaghan

Washington Old Hall

The ancestral home of George Washington, Washington Old Hall was constructed in the twelfth century, with William de Hertburne taking possession of the hall and lands before 1183 and changing his name to William de Wessyngton. The Washington family, as they became known, spent the next four and a half centuries at Washington Old Hall before moving to Sulgrave Manor in Northamptonshire, at which point the Old Hall was sold to the Bishop of Durham.

The hall remained a residence until the nineteenth century when it was converted into tenement flats, falling into such disrepair that by the 1930s it was declared unfit for human habitation and scheduled for demolition. Local teacher Fred Hall founded what is now the Friends of the Old Hall to rescue the building and campaign for its restoration, which was finally completed in 1955. The building was transferred to the National Trust in 1957. Twenty years later, in 1977, Jimmy Carter became the first American President to visit the Old Hall, famously planting a tree with his counterpart Prime Minister James Callaghan. Washington Old Hall remains one of the most fascinating historic attractions in the North East, and hosts an annual Independence Day celebration every July 4. Because of its historic links to George Washington, the Hall has been a major feature of Sunderland's Sister-City relationship with Washington DC, the only non-capital in the world to have such a relationship with the American capital. Visitors from the States are often surprised to find that Washington DC's flag is actually the coat of arms of George's ancestors from Washington, Tyne and Wear.

Hylton Castle

Many years ago, Hylton Castle stood guard over a ferry crossing at the River Wear. It was built by William De Hylton around 1400 and was occupied until the early twentieth century. The Hylton family were wealthy and had estates in Yorkshire, Durham and Northumberland and by the 13th century had assumed the title of a barony within the Bishopric of Durham. The castle reflected the Hylton family's status and the family kept its rank and wealth until the Civil War. Even later the family were prosperous enough to refurbish the interior and add wings to the north and south side of the gatehouse in the first half of the 18th century. After the last member of the Hylton family died in 1746, the estate was sold, later to be bought by a local man, William Briggs, who demolished the 18th century wings, added larger windows and rebuilt the interior.

The castle became famous for a ghost called the 'Cauld Lad o' Hylton'. The ghost was the spirit of a stable boy killed by a lord of Hylton in the 1500s. The boy's ghost sometimes carried his head under his arm and was occasionally seen and often heard by servants at the castle. He liked to throw dishes and plates around the castle's kitchen after it had been tidied. Sometimes he pretended to be a ferryman and after charging people to cross the river, he would leave them stranded in the middle.

Today Hylton Castle still retains some of the original features of the castle, in particular, the stone-carved coats of arms. These arms can be seen around the castle walls and represent various important local families who have lived in the area in the past, including shields of the Hylton, Lumley, Percy, Grey and Eure families and of the Washington family who lived nearby.

Recently the Heritage Lottery Fund made a significant award to Hylton Castle and with match funding from Sunderland City Council will transform the 14th century castle from an empty shell into a living, working building that benefits the local community and visitors. This project will bring an important part of Sunderland's heritage back in to use, safeguarding the long-term future of this Scheduled Ancient Monument. As an educational, community and visitor attraction the castle will enable current and future generations to discover its rich history and heritage.

Richard Callaghan 255

A Recent History Of Music In Sunderland

WORDS BY *Ross Millard*

Musician, Artist and
Artistic Director

A Recent History
Of Music
In Sunderland

"The Royalty pub on Chester Road (now the Stumble Inn) was the venue of choice"

I should say that this chapter merely serves as a rough guide to what I believe to be some key happenings in the Sunderland music scene over the last 20 years or so. To give full respect to individuals who at one time have, or still are organising, promoting and working on music in the City would require much more space than this chapter will allow. With this in mind, I've chosen to concentrate on a few key moments over the last couple of decades, on which to drape some finer details, in a bid to explain how we come to make music in this City.

When the late John Peel came to Sunderland during the filming of his 1999 Channel 4 series 'Sounds of the Suburbs', he found a City in the aftermath of a 'revolution we didn't want' - a post-industrial 'graveyard' where music seemed to be the only salvation for a section of the teen populace.

So charmed by the Bunker, still standing (and in fact thriving) some 17 years on, he donated significant funds to help keep the rehearsal rooms open in the face of public-

funding cutbacks. Such a display of public support, you could argue, was a pre-cursor to the affection and attention that music industry outsiders would pay to the City over the course of the next 15 years.

Of course, John Peel was often charmed by young people ploughing their own furrow, and we see in the programme how he takes great pleasure in discovering local band Comatose rehearsing in the Bunker whilst he explores the narrow, noisy corridors of the building. He offers the band a session on his Radio1 show, at that time one of the station's most loved regular slots, and a pinnacle achievement on any indie-band's bucket list. Hazel, singer of the group, with dyed peach hair and an SG guitar covered in stickers, appears to not know what he's talking about. How's that for ploughing your own furrow, John? He's duly charmed. Welcome to Sunderland.

I was 17 in 1999, and beginning to explore some pathways of my own into the local music scene. At that time, The

Royalty pub on Chester Road (now the Stumble Inn) was the venue of choice for any would-be bands and musicians. With a lack of any bona-fide, purpose built music venues in the City, the Royalty offered young people the opportunity to hire out their upstairs function room, and with the addition of a small vocal PA, suddenly there was the chance to create a modest but regular haunt for anyone in the city who wanted to play their own songs to a small but devoted audience every Friday or Saturday night.

It was at the Royalty that I first met James McMahon, or James Jam, as he was known by his 'fanzine name' back in those days. James was a fresher at Sunderland Uni – he'd come to the city from Doncaster, another town that was on the brink of a post-industrial slump. James had started to organise regular events at the Royalty, under the name 'Boyeater'. The premise of James' gigs was simple. Find anyone he could who showed even a passing interest in the underground DIY indie-rock of the time, and encourage them all to either form bands, pick up instruments or just turn up at the pub as a keen spectator. This basic, lovable corralling did the trick and it really wasn't long before a handful of bands had formed in Sunderland simply because of these Boyeater shows and James' infectious personality. Add to that existing groups of the time such as Lucas

Renney and Neil Bassett's 'Brilliantine', and Dave Brewis' 'New Tellers', and Sunderland was already bubbling up to becoming an interesting place for emerging music.

Chester Road was, and still is, one of the main streets for student accommodation in the City, and the Royalty acted as a fairly sensible nexus for any music-loving gig-goers. I was studying for my A-levels at Bede college at the time, but I'd chanced upon one of James' gigs at the Royalty one night and I instantly recognised that he had a similar outlook on performance and musicality as myself. That is, that it's far better to just get up and have a go than spend agonising amounts of time in your bedroom fretting over learning more chords or playing more notes, faster. There was a freedom in James' philosophy, and I wanted in.

At the same time, SCCDYP (Sunderland City Centre Detached Youth Project) was reaching what felt like critical mass. Every Saturday morning, without fail, kids from all corners of the City would descend on The Bunker for a few hours to rehearse, write music and generally associate with other like-minded individuals. These sessions were the idea of Dave Murray, a wonderful youth worker who had a huge passion for music.

I turned up for the first time with Jaff (later we'd go on to form The Futureheads together) and a couple of other friends

A Recent History Of Music In Sunderland

from college. We already had a little band going, and we'd heard that you could get free rehearsal time at The Bunker on a Saturday morning. When we got there, we realised that something else took precedence over band practice – collaboration. Dave placed great emphasis on the kids forming temporary bands and groups to write songs about the popular issues of the day – little didactic vignettes such as 'The Condom Song', '(Do You) Sniff Glue', and others. Looking back, this was an effective way of getting kids, who are quite often introspective, to collaborate and perform together. No easy task, but Dave was a master at it. Friendships blossomed, bands were formed, and the project was a huge success until its unfortunate relocation to the Hendon YMCA in the year 2000.

It was at these Saturday morning SCCDYP sessions that I first met Barry and Dave Hyde (also erstwhile Futureheads), and Dave and Peter Brewis. They were all regulars at the youth workshop sessions. We all had a deep love of music, but our taste was vast and eclectic. Barry and Dave had the spoils of their father Fred's enormous record collection. Dave

punk-rock band fronted by Frankie Stubbs.

Leatherface achieved legendary cult status on the punk circuit, especially in the US, where I believe they (Frankie Stubbs and guitarist Dickie Hammond) paved the way for a guitar style of muted arpeggio picking and chugging that you can now hear on countless releases from many American punk record labels. They are fairly unsung originators of an entire genre, in my view.

Frankie and Dickie could often be seen at The Royalty, taking a look at what new talent was coming through, and on one night in May 2001 two worlds finally came together as Leatherface played a hometown show at The Alexandria in Grangetown, with Floridians Hot Water Music and James McMahon's Sunderland-based band Mavis as support. A significant moment, in the sense that it was the first time in my memory that I'd seen a local band play to a crowd of 300+ people (with an American support band as well! Unthinkable). In hindsight, I think that show raised the bar over what could be possible, in many, many ways.

Also conceived in Sunderland was Slampt Records – a

"Friendships blossomed, bands were formed, and the project was a huge success until its unfortunate relocation to the Hendon YMCA"

and Peter Brewis were already seasoned musicians who had played actual gigs on the more traditional 'pub and social club' circuit with their first band, The Underfoot. I was a total nerd for noisy, guitar-based punk-rock. I remember trading Barry a Pavement record for Nick Drake's 'Five Leaves Left' – we were all discovering, experimenting – it was a great time to be starting a band in the City.

Alongside the SCCDYP sessions at The Bunker, other notable hangouts for local musicians at the time included Hot Rats records, ran by ex-Toy Dolls member Marty Yule and Sound World, a local guitar shop that sold the basic supplies that anyone looking to start a band could possibly need. These three hotspots formed a bit of a 'golden triangle' around Park Lane bus station, and were often packed full of teens on any given Saturday.

That isn't to say that even the recent history of music in Sunderland should start in 1999. The pre-cursor to this DIY indie flame could be laid squarely at the door of two pre-eminent 1990's groups from the City; namely Kenickie (Sunderland's first post-Dave Stewart music-industry success story), and Leatherface, a hugely influential underground

fiercely DIY record label that channelled the counter-cultural spirit of Olympia, Washington and, for an all too brief moment, made a big name for itself in the underground world of collectible vinyl and cult, post-riot grrrl rock.

Slampt was a label started in the mid-nineties by Dover-born, Sunderland University-educated Pete Dale. The blueprint for Slampt was embedded in the DIY culture of US-based 'bedroom' labels like Kill Rock Stars from Olympia, Washington, or Teenbeat from Washington DC – record labels with the philosophy of documenting bands and performers based on raw aesthetic and politics; in Slampt's case, feminism, independence and at times, anarchism. Although Pete moved the label quite swiftly to a new HQ in Newcastle, where it thrived for many years, the seeds were planted in Sunderland, and when Kenickie emerged in 1994/95, Slampt moved quickly to release the group's early music.

Marie Nixon (formerly Marie Du Santiago) explains how Kenickie came into being, and how the landscape of mid-nineties Brit-pop propelled them toward the nations capital:

"In Sunderland, 1994, Emma, Lauren and Marie (that's me), motivated by a powerful love of music and each other, formed a band. We picked up guitars and microphones, and asked Lauren's brother Peter, a stalwart of the eternally lively Sunderland music scene, to join us on drums as we spent sunny days holed up in an attic discovering powerchords and which way up to hold the guitars while writing songs describing our school, our town, our lives and each other.

Between that day and our eventual break up just four short years later we signed to EMI and Warner Brothers, released two albums, two Peel sessions for the BBC, were in the top 10 and on Top of the Pops. Rimmel even named an eyeliner after us – high praise indeed. Throughout this, intentionally and otherwise, our creativity and the imagery associated with us was forged and shaped by our home town of Sunderland.

We sang in our own accents and wrote songs in the Sunderland vernacular.

In our dress we aimed for the glamour of the greatest Sunderland nights out, rejecting the dour 90's uniform of cargo pants, plaid shirts and stringy, over straightened hair, in favour of glitter and fake fur, sparkly heels and tight skirts that put us in mind of our most glamourous aunties in their heyday – dancing to Roxy Music out on the Sunderland town on the Saturday night of their lives.

All of this was a bit confusing for the national media, who sometimes superimposed their ideas of the north and northern women over us. In interviews our quotes would be littered with swearwords we hadn't uttered, with a mise en scene of caricatured working class culture, pints and chips and cigarette fug. For a period it was as if all our photoshoots were to be conducted in front of some urban decay, as a means of quite literally locating us in a national narrative about Sunderland and its post-industrial decline. Because of this we cherished the company of a clever music press and advocates like John Peel. They saw us; young but not dumb, loud but not thoughtless, made up but fiercely feminist, fun but deadly serious about music, politics, what I now understand to be the transformational power of creativity. The Sunderland live music scene initially struggled to take us to their hearts - from the perspective of some of our contemporaries we couldn't play and hadn't paid our dues to the scene, and they probably didn't recognise the Sunderland they loved as reported back through many of our broadsheet interviews – we certainly didn't. The ease of our transition from avid gig goers to a bonafide, successful indie band with stickers of their faces cover-mounted on Smash Hits caused some discomfort. I looked on with envy and joy at the supportive, open scene created in Sunderland just a few years later which allowed bands like Field Music and The Futureheads to flourish, and it's deeply satisfying that

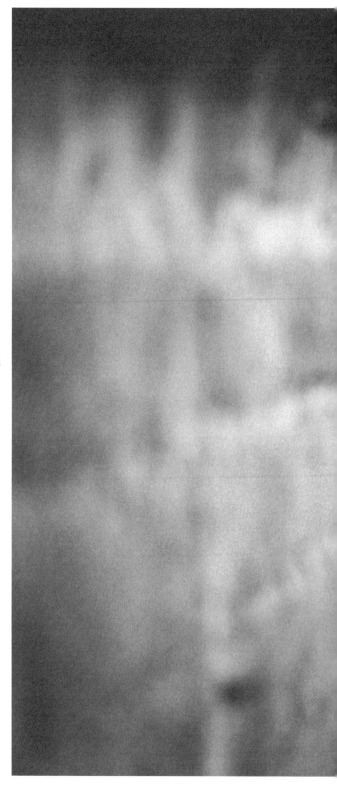

A Recent History Of Music In Sunderland

Ross Millard

THIS AIN'T VEGAS

one of the ring-leaders of that welcoming, woman-friendly Sunderland scene, James McMahon, cites Kenickie as an important band for him".

The Futureheads formed in the autumn of 2000, in the aftermath of Dave Murray's youth project. The band began with an initial line-up of Barry Hyde, Jaff (David Craig), Peter Brewis (later of Field Music), and myself. After several months of rehearsing in a freezing garage that belonged to Barry's parents, we played our first gig in the Ditchburn Suite at Ashbrooke Cricket Club in December 2000. By this time, the cricket club had become the most often-used music venue in the City, and gigs would be held there on a regular basis. Richard Amundsen, founder of the well-loved, seminal This Ain't Vegas started 'Beats Happening', named in tribute to the fiercely DIY, US-based indie-punk stalwarts Beat Happening. Like James before him, Richard looked to bring in bands from around the country and beyond, mirroring collectives like Double Down from Newcastle, and the thriving DIY scene in Leeds at that time. As Dave Brewis of Field Music explained in a blog he wrote for The Guardian in May 2012: 'This Ain't Vegas were the kind of band who

inspired devotion and, more so, they inspired other bands to form. Not only that but TAV (as everybody knew them) made links with bands from other cities and dragged them north to play Beats Happening nights alongside the merry-go-round of newly-minted Sunderland bands'.

In all honesty, back in '01/'02 The Futureheads were happy with our lot as an active band on the local circuit – keen to play as much as possible, but with no great ambitions toward record deals and world tours. That 'blue sky thinking' didn't often come into conversation with bands in the North-East at this time; other than Kenickie, there was no real precedent for music-industry interest in anything that was happening north of Wetherby services, to be honest. We were too busy trying to make each gig a one-off; painting our faces silver and pretending to be robots, or performing our small repertoire to a backing tape, karaoke-style. Still, fate has a funny way of brewing up trouble and in an out-of-the-blue phone conversation, Pete Dale (Slampt, Milky Wimpshake, Red Monkey) offered the remaining four spaces in the Milky Wimpshake van to The Futureheads for their forthcoming summer 2002 European Tour. Flattered -

"I looked on with envy and joy at the supportive, open scene created in Sunderland in just a few years"

honoured, even, we confirmed the trip and jumped headfirst into the exciting world of touring. At this juncture, Peter (our drummer at the time) thought it best that he stay behind in Sunderland and concentrate on his own band, Field Music, and between us we agreed to get Dave Hyde behind the kit as a solution. That decision turned out in everyone's favour as Peter was beginning work on what became the first, brilliant, Field Music record with his brother David, and we struck on the line-up that would eventually see us record five studio albums and regularly tour around the world for over a decade. We've always stayed close friends, and we continued to share

a rehearsal/studio space together on Swan Street in Monkwearmouth for many years throughout the 00's.

At the time of our first album release in mid-2004, the NME ran an article on the top UK Cities for music. Sunderland was sitting proudly in the top 5. John Kennedy, XFM DJ and champion of new music wrote in Dazed and Confused magazine 'All roads lead to Sunderland. We've had Detroit, New York, Berlin, London and Liverpool, now it's time to make way for Sunderland'.

I remember being tickled by the Sunderland Echo running a confusing headline around the same time,

proclaiming 'Sunderland is the new Manchester'. Weird, but it strangely encapsulated the positivity around music in the City at that time. I think a copy of the paper still proudly hangs in Kenny Sanger's manager's office in The Bunker to this day.

BBC Radio 1 brought their 'Big Weekend' to Sunderland in 2005, and The Futureheads were asked to headline their second stage above New Yorker's Interpol. Herrington Country Park was filled with household names like Foo Fighters, Gwen Stefani and The Chemical Brothers. It was beginning to feel like the tide was turning. Attention was coming. We made it on to the cover of the NME, our debut record achieved Gold status and we were touring all over the world.

By the mid-00's, more groups were forming, local promoter and businessman Ben Wall had opened Bar 36 on Holmeside, and organisers such as Dave Harper, David Littlefair, Carly Davidson and Dan Shannon were continuing the work that people like James McMahon and Richard Amundsen had done previously in bringing many bands to the region. Suddenly agents were sending exciting new bands to Sunderland. Bloc Party, The Zutons, Snow Patrol and many more played in the city during this period, alongside cult bands such as Strike Anywhere, Send More Paramedics and Lemuria.

Split Festival came along in 2009, initially as a fundraiser to aid the ailing Ashbrooke Cricket Club. The organising team was sizeable (all four of The Futureheads, local music

A Recent History Of Music In Sunderland

promoters/businessmen Martyn McFadden and Rob Deverson, and This Ain't Vegas' Richard Amundsen). The main aim was to get a medium/large-scale event off the ground in the City. For five all-too-brief years, Split Festival offered Sunderland an outdoor summertime live music event to rival other cities in the North-East, featuring artists such as Public Image Ltd, The Charlatans, Dizzee Rascal, Beth Orton, The Unthanks and more.

Split expanded from a one-day event to two days quickly, and gathered some momentum, winning a North East Culture Award for Best Event Sunderland in 2011. Audience figures unfortunately plateaued around the 3000 mark, though, and finally, in 2014, Split Festival relocated from the Ashbrooke Cricket Club site to Mowbray Park in the centre of town for one last hurrah. In the five years that Split was around, the associated costs of running a festival had spiraled to the point of insanity. As musicians and performers sought to make more of their overall income from live performance, the fees and negotiations with live agents meant that the talent budget for the festival had to be well in excess of £100k, and when added to the costs of infrastructure, production and marketing etc., it's evident that running a festival takes serious cash. Arts Council England and Sunderland City Council really backed Split Festival for our last event in 2014, but perhaps the timing was just a little out of line with what was to come for the City, and the audience just didn't quite exist at that moment in time.

A Recent History Of Music In Sunderland

"We made it on to the cover of the NME, our debut record achieved Gold status and we were touring all over the world."

We were enthusiasts first and promoters second, and in that climate, with a limited audience, we just couldn't quite balance the books.

Split Festival is survived, in a way, by Summer Streets Festival – a Cultural Spring-based event that takes place on the north side of Sunderland every July. Also, in the last couple of years, Sunniside Live has had some success in bringing outdoor live music back into the City Centre.

In December 2008, Frankie & The Heartstrings played their first gig at Independent (which was Bar 36, renamed).

In the space of 10 more shows, they'd be signed to Wichita Recordings, and have a 7" single released on Rough Trade, counting the influential Geoff Travis, and legendary producer/DJ Andrew Weatherall as fans. A sign of the times, in part, as to how the gears of the music industry had quickened, but also an indicator that music in the North-East was now on the nation's radar.

The early success of the Heartstrings, alongside the demise of the physical retail side of the music industry, led to the band opening Pop Recs Ltd in June 2012, in what used to be the tourist information office on Fawcett Street. Anne Tye, of Sunderland City Council, assisted tremendously in the establishing of the space. The shop was intended to serve as a record store, performance space and gallery, and act as a comment on the demise of the record store as we know it. However, with a flurry of surprise guest performances from the likes of The Cribs, Edwyn Collins and Franz Ferdinand, Pop Recs Ltd quickly began to serve a whole new purpose, as drummer and proprietor Dave Harper explains: 'Pop Recs was a place which was able to evolve, move and adapt quickly

to cultural changes in the area, to showcase and develop local talent and most importantly act as a safe, non-judgmental, creative hub for everyone.

'Pop Recs, like many things in Sunderland was born out of adversity. Despite attracting household names such as James Bay, The Vaccines, Maximo Park, The Futureheads, The Charlatans et al, Pop Recs was forced to close its doors in early 2015 as the building that housed us was sold for redevelopment. After a successful crowd funding campaign (raising £14k through the Kickstarter website), Pop Recs Ltd reopened on Stockton Road in November 2015. Michael McKnight (also of Frankie & The Heartstrings) and myself continue to facilitate poetry nights, a mental health support drop-in, songwriting workshops (with New Writing North), host gallery space, serve coffee, sell records and other associated creative folly'.

In the couple of years since Split Festival's demise, it's striking how much more frequently musicians in the city are working in partnership with other organisations. Back in 2010, even, the Arts Council was rarely part of the vocabulary of an emerging musician or band. Connections between artists and the City Council or the University didn't really exist. The MAC Trust and the idea of the Fire Station becoming a venue was yet to emerge. As infrastructural plans develop, and the relationships between artists and organisations continue to grow, Sunderland is laying the foundations toward a prolific few years. Summer Streets Festival, the Asunder project (featuring Field Music and the RNS), and the various Sunderland City of Culture 2021 live events are seeing to that. Sunderland band Lilliput have

opened their own coffee shop on Holmeside, and they are also actively scheduling and promoting live music in the City, alongside the continuing work of Pop Recs Ltd.

Martin Longstaff's The Lake Poets project has blossomed in this time, and in 2015 he released his debut album to much critical acclaim. Recorded in Nashville under the tutelage of Sunderland-born Dave Stewart, The Lake Poets is one of the latest offerings from Wearside's musical production line, and in working on the record with Dave Stewart offers a nice full-circle ending on what is only the tip of the iceberg in terms of the modern-day musical adventures of our City.

With the Fire Station venue having been green-lit by Arts Council, the next five years could be really significant in terms of the emergence of the next wave of musicians and performers from Sunderland. The infrastructure is changing, and long-standing, important organisations like The Bunker

are now supported by newer projects and initiatives like Pop Recs Ltd and Sunderland's 2021 City of Culture bid. Huge concerts at the Stadium of Light are bringing more gig-goers than ever before to the City, whilst independent promoters are still working hard to keep live music happening, regardless of space, time and money. Music in the Minster are bringing opera into the City, Keith Gregson is a strong advocate for folk music in the City Centre, and there are regular blues music events in town thanks to George Shovlin now, too.

Field Music's Mercury Music Prize nomination for their 'Plumb' record in 2012 was seen by many in Sunderland as an overdue nod to their significance on a national scale, but as Marie Nixon says: 'Sunderland knows now more than ever before how valuable, vital and singular its creative culture is'.

It seems like we're also more comfortable celebrating these days.

SUMMER STREETS

First held in 2014, Summer Streets is commissioned by the Cultural Spring and is a celebration of a rich variety of musical genres. Bringing an eclectic mix of community artists and well renowned names to a neighbourhood park in Southwick in Sunderland over a weekend in mid-July, it has become a regular fixture in the city's cultural calendar, offering the opportunity for people across the city to enjoy a whole range of musical genres, from opera and jazz to bluegrass and pop.

Creative Director Ross Millard, singer and guitarist for The

Futureheads and Frankie and the Heartstrings, programmes the festival and aims to introduce audiences to new types of music as well as creating a platform for new and emerging local talent, and more established, recognised bands and artists. Ross's eclectic programmes have included rock bands, jazz musicians, dance groups, choir groups, bluegrass, drumming groups, tea dance bands and opera workshops. The programmes have also included opportunities for people to play an instrument for the first time through

classes and workshops.

The festival opens with performers parading through the streets of Southwick, with flag wavers and musicians giving a lively, colourful taste of the weekend ahead.

Alongside the music, Summer Streets also includes a variety of other artistic forms, and offers opportunities for local schools and community groups to get directly involved in the festival including artwork and decorations made by local children.

After attracting about 4,000 people in 2014 it has gone from strength to strength. In 2015, headlined by Hyde and Beast, the festival was held over two days, with the Sunday having an Alice in Wonderland theme. Ross Millard again programmed an amazing, eclectic mix of musical genres that was thoroughly enjoyed by 5,000 people. Held for the third time in 2016 the festival attracted an estimated 8,000 people who enjoyed a weekend of live music that included the premiere of a Cultural Spring research and development project, Putting the Band Back Together.

The event, hosted as usual by the BBC's Jeff Brown and Ray Spencer from the Customs House, was headlined by Field Music and included performances from the Royal Northern Sinfonia, The Cornshed Sisters, indie band Martha and the Heavenly Thrillbillies.

Summer Streets has won a number of awards and is now seen as one of the best annual cultural events in Sunderland.

Summer Streets

First held in 2014, Summer Streets is commissioned by the Cultural Spring and is a celebration of a rich variety of musical genres. Bringing an eclectic mix of community artists and well renowned names to a neighbourhood park in Southwick in Sunderland over a weekend in mid-July, it has become a regular fixture in the city's cultural calendar, offering the opportunity for people across the city to enjoy a whole range of musical genres, from opera and jazz to bluegrass and pop.

Creative Director Ross Millard, singer and guitarist for The Futureheads and Frankie and the Heartstrings, programmes the festival and aims to introduce audiences to new types of music as well as creating a platform for new and emerging local talent, and more established, recognised bands and artists. Ross's eclectic programmes have included rock bands, jazz musicians, dance groups, choir groups, bluegrass, drumming groups, tea dance bands and opera workshops. The programmes have also included opportunities for people to play an instrument for the first time through classes and workshops.

The festival opens with performers parading through the streets of Southwick, with flag wavers and musicians giving a lively, colourful taste of the weekend ahead.

Alongside the music, Summer Streets also includes a variety of other artistic forms, and offers opportunities for local schools and community groups to get directly involved in the festival including artwork and decorations made by local children.

After attracting about 4,000 people in 2014 it has gone from strength to strength. In 2015, headlined by Hyde and Beast, the festival was held over two days, with the Sunday having an Alice in Wonderland theme. Ross Millard again programmed an amazing, electric mix of musical genres that was thoroughly enjoyed by 5,000 people. Held for the third time in 2016 the festival attracted an estimated 8,000 people who enjoyed a weekend of live music which included the premiere of a Cultural Spring research and development project, Putting the Band Back Together. The event, hosted as usual by the BBC's Jeff Brown and Ray Spencer from the Customs House, was headlined by Field Music and included performances from the Royal Northern Sinfonia, The Cornshed Sisters, indie band Martha and the Heavenly Thrillbillies. The 2017 event included some of the North-East's best live bands such as Frankie and the Heartstrings, Warm Digits and the Oompah Brass Band and as well as the music there were loads of hands-on workshops and kids entertainment Summer Streets has won a number of awards and is now seen as one of the best annual cultural events in Sunderland.

Richard Callaghan

New Writing In Sunderland

WORDS BY *IAIN ROWAN*
Holmeside Writers.

New Writing In Sunderland

"The writers' group has literally changed my life."

We started Holmeside Writers with a simple idea: a writers group that would be accessible, free and devoted to creative writing in its broadest sense. The owners of the newly-opened Holmeside Coffee wanted to make it more than just another cafe, and had already developed plans for a book club and film club, and were looking for an idea that would complement that growing cultural hub - and so Holmeside Writers was born.

We advertised this new group, planned the first meeting for February 2014, and hoped that we might get three or four interested people along and grow it from there.

On a cold, wet February night, eleven people came to the first meeting.

Many of those people are still coming now, over two years on. Nearly seventy people belong to the group's virtual meeting place on Facebook, and it's not uncommon to have twenty people at a meeting. Within a year, demand was such that a second date each month was added to the calendar. It's perhaps informative to hear the voices of some of the members on what the group means to them, why they come, why they have stayed, and how it has developed their writing:

"The writers' group has literally changed my life." (Hester)

"Now I feel so confident that I now teach my own creative writing class...it turned me from an amateur writer into a professional writer." (Tom)

"My world has always been building and football, which can be unforgivingly masculine, and there was a part of me that wanted to encounter, and be part of, something collectively creative...have gone from being happy writing a couple of pages to now concentrating on writing my first novel." (Ray)

"This has given me the confidence to leave my well paid office job to become a full time writer." (Alan)

"As a writer, Holmeside has made me a writer again! I now dedicate much more time to writing and consequently enjoy it a lot more. It has also opened my eyes to opportunities that I can apply for to improve my writing and potentially get it out there." (Lisa)

The membership reflects the aim to explore a wide notion of creative writing, and includes novelists (published, and working towards publication), short story writers, playwrights and screenwriters and radio dramatists, poets (traditional and performance), graphic novelists, bloggers and successful non-fiction authors, and many members who are not committed to any particular form but just enjoy trying out new ways of writing and developing their skills. The group serves those who are serious about publication, but also those who write for pure enjoyment of the craft and creativity.

We have ranged far and wide in our exploration of creative writing, discussing and working on traditional subjects of writing groups, discussing short stories and novels, narrative and dialogue, character development and point of view, but also hosting workshops on radio drama, non-fiction, short plays and performance, blogging, innovative and creative approaches to publishing fiction in an online world, and we continue to look for new ways to explore creative approaches to writing, and to learning about writing.

"All of the activity of the group has been achieved with no funding, with all contributions on a voluntary basis"

We draw on the expert input of others, for example hosting workshops on writing for performance from a regional performance poet, and from an award-winning American writer/actor/director who was staging a show in Sunderland the day after our meeting. We also try to grow and develop our own experience as a group, to promote confidence and skills development amongst our members. In the past few months they have led workshops on radio drama, on blogging, and on how to avoid defamation in non-fiction and fiction. Members are now contributing to the development of new writing beyond our group: one runs a writers' workshop with clients of the charity MIND, another is delivering workshops on self-publishing. Members have been published for the first time, been placed as runners-up in national competitions, published books, won awards – but we all also take great satisfaction when a new member reads their work to others for the first time, or sends off their first piece to a competition or publisher. Informal peer support and critique groups have developed:

"Three of the group have met with me privately to discuss a talk I was invited to give. They shared their own experiences of confidence building and public speaking. Their advice has been invaluable." (Glenda)

"The main benefit of being involved with the group has been the friendships and the building of trusting relationships. Having people, whose ability as writers you respect and admire, read your work and give back strong constructive criticism has been the main driving force in the improvement in my writing." (Ray)

All of the activity of the group has been achieved with no funding, with all contributions on a voluntary basis, and with the support of Holmeside Coffee/Independent who provide the venue for free simply because they think it is an important and worthwhile thing to do. This is not unique for us, and is typical of the cultural scene in Sunderland and its culture of co-operation and collaboration.

Cuckoo Young Writers group in Sunderland was established in September 2014. It is one of a number of young writers' groups which New Writing North run across the North East (Cuckoo Young Writers is the name of the NWN young writers programme), all established with the aim of ensuring that all young people in the region have access to a weekly on-going group where they can take their work, be introduced to new styles of writing and meet other young writers.

Establishing a group in Sunderland was a very important milestone for Cuckoo Young Writers for the obvious reasons: Sunderland is a big city, with a thriving cultural scene, but very little provision for young people, and young writers in particular. However, it took some time, as securing funding that would be long- term and not project-based (something which is surprisingly difficult, as most funders prefer "events" and one-off projects rather than on-going work) was difficult. Identifying a suitable place to hold the sessions was also tricky. Cuckoo prefer to keep the groups out of "institutions" (libraries, colleges etc.) and instead hold them in cultural spaces, and because of the lack of arts spaces in Sunderland, it took for Pop Recs to open for Cuckoo in Sunderland to find a natural home.

Since funding has been secured (and is now until July 2017), the group has been challenging in a number of ways. Although the initial intention was to start with song writing

Iain Rowan

281

New Writing In Sunderland

poets and combining that with an open mic slot which has enabled many people to read their work out aloud to others for the first time. King Ink is hosted by the record shop/cafe/cultural hub PopRecs, who provide the space and support for free because they see it as being an important part of what they do. PopRecs itself, in its present form, was largely funded by an astonishingly successful crowd-funding campaign - and so the people of Sunderland interested in supporting grassroots culture raise funds to allow a cultural hub to keep running which in turn allows groups like King Ink to have a home, and the people of Sunderland (and beyond) to hear and read and develop their poetry. This is culture from the grassroots, supportive and collaborative, and the people of Sunderland making space and opportunities for themselves.

King Ink was founded in 2014 by Sunderland poets Brian Anderson and Patrick Shannon to provide a performance poetry and prose platform for writers in the City of Sunderland, particularly to those who did not have a forum to present emerging works. They setup a monthly reading group where original works could be presented, and explored. In two years King Ink has become a vibrant community arts group. Supportive publishers and other published poets from across the region attend and perform regularly and encourage new and emerging writers to present material. This has led to the emergence of new writers across the city, the publication of poets locally by both Mudfog Press and Red Squirrel Press,

and inter-arts partnerships and cross-city alliances (such as the 'All We Are Saying' arts exhibition in Sunderland Minster in September 2015). King Ink writers have presented works across the North East to audiences at Darlington Literary Festival, the Literary and Philosophical Society, the Teesside Literary Festival, and Gateshead Writers group. A dozen new publications have been launched or read at King Ink, and the group is working towards producing its own first anthology. All of this has been achieved organically, without funding or formal structures. It is likely that in order to achieve its further objectives that King Ink will develop formal structures, in the nature of a social enterprise. The challenge for the future is to sustain the group as a writing force for new and original poetry and prose.

Another new venture in 2016 was the establishment of Slam!, a performance poetry night founded on the success of the University of Sunderland students in student poetry slam events, and run by a member of the University's creative writing team. In another illustration of the way groups within the city link and mutually support one another, the founder of Slam! is also a member of Holmeside Writers and its inaugural event was attended by members of both Holmeside Writers and King Ink. There is no sense of there being competition between groups or projects; people involved in all of these promote each other with as much energy as they

"Over the past eighteen months, the group King Ink has established itself as a safe and friendly environment for people to hear and read poetry"

New Writing In Sunderland

do their own interests: there is a feeling that we are all part of the common good, and what strengthens one part of the Sunderland cultural scene benefits the rest.

"What has struck me about Sunderland is the amount of creative energy at work within the city and the university has been attempting to build and develop that energy and nurture the distinctive talent in the area. This year we started Slam!, a poetry and performance night at Holmeside Writers. The night attracted over 80 people and felt like a wonderful collaborative evening between established writers from other groups and long-running events, such as Jibba Jabba and King Ink, university creative writing students, interested members of the public and previous students who have moved on but returned to give performances. From this night we were lucky enough to establish a link with Apples and Snakes who are now running a pilot night of Scratch Newcastle, which has been running for 5 years under the mentorship of Kirstin Luckins. The scheme is for all writers within the Sunderland region, students and the local community, and is another exciting attempt to give a voice and a developmental platform to writers in the area. David Wares, who hosts the jazz show on Spark FM is featuring recorded work from writers who performed at the Slam! night on his radio show."

(Founder of Slam, Dr. Sarah Dobbs, herself a published novelist)

In addition, in January 2016 Sarah and the University launched the first 'University of Sunderland in association with Waterstones Short Story Award'. The award has so far attracted a lot of interest and again hopes to spark awareness of the distinctive voices and particular identities from within the region and beyond.

One of the aims for Holmeside Writers has always been to take creative writing beyond the confines of our own group, and to do interesting work in interesting places with other creative people, to collaborate and experiment.

Sometimes this means being brave and spontaneous, and being prepared to step out of our comfort zones. An example of this was our 2015 collaboration with the Northern Gallery for Contemporary Art, and their exhibiting artist Beatriz Olabarrieta. Beatriz wanted to work with local writers to develop creative writing in response to her work, but to do so spontaneously in and around the artwork itself, with no pre-planning or preconceived ideas. Volunteers from Holmeside Writers met in the gallery with Beatriz and Kathryn Brame from the NGCA who had brokered the idea, and a whole day of writing and creativity evolved from there. The participants developed a character who had come into the gallery, and then put in them in motion, interacting with and reacting to the art. The group came back together, sat in the centre of the

New Writing In Sunderland

gallery, and read out their work, and then retreated once again to desks placed around and in the art and developed their character's reaction to the others. By repeating this iterative process of creation and discussion throughout the day, fascinating and original narratives evolved.

Some of the participants went on to write reviews of Beatriz's work, and this is echoed by a new collaboration with the NGCA. In association with the Arts Council funded Cuckoo Young Writers, the NGCA is running a series of five workshops called Reviewers In Residence, linked to the NGCA exhibition 'Baldock Pope Zahle', and aimed at young writers/ artists (aged 15-23 and based in the North of England) who want to gain more confidence or experience in writing about or reviewing contemporary art exhibitions. Members of Holmeside Writers are leading two of those workshops, including a workshop on using the techniques of writing fiction inspired by artwork as a way in to analysing emotional reactions to art that can then provide a way in to thinking about reviewing that art.

The groups have close links with the University of

In October 2016 we brought some of the supporters of writing in Sunderland together to stage our first ever Festival of Creative Writing. Sunderland Library Services had run a Literature Festival for a few years, and an early positive discussion made the decision to collaborate: although the two festivals would be programmed organised separately, we would brand it to the public as one Sunderland Festival of Literature and Creative Writing. The writing side of the festival was a collaboration between Iain Rowan, acting as creative director, and Hannah Matterson and Kristian Foreman from the MAC Trust, which provided the resources needed to stage the Festival. We worked closely with the Libraries Service and the University of Sunderland's Department of Culture, which contributed many events to the Literature side, and this co-operation and collaboration is an example of that mutual support that exists throughout the city - the creative writing team handled the website and social media presence for the two strands, and Library Services likewise oversaw the production of the combined print brochure.

> "I think the group already sits well within the culture and artistic development in the city, being linked with events such as spoken word"

Sunderland and in particular its creative writing team and their students. An example is a recent project that saw creative writing students collecting stories of the strange and supernatural from people in communities across Wearside. This research was then turned into a number of story topics that writers could pitch for, and a number of Holmeside Writers (among others) pitched and were then given commissions to write short stories or poetry based on the original legends. The creative writing students are running a professional process of selection, editing, design and eventually publication in an anthology.

All of the groups mentioned see themselves as part of a wider cultural network, across practices and art forms, and for some of their members it has been a gateway into involvement in the city's cultural eco-system:

"One thing led to another and now I am engaging with creative people in Sunderland through inspirational networks and groups (such as ArtWorksU and King Ink) that until a few months ago I didn't even know existed." (Blaine)

"I think the group already sits well within the culture and artistic development in the city, being linked with events such as spoken word, or community focal points such as the library service." (Lisa)

We established a set of principles for our creative writing festival early with three themes: accessibility, diversity of programming, and combining national-impact experience with local talent.

In order to make the festival as accessible as possible we ran it across an entire month, with events at different times of day and on weekends as well as in the week, and we made all events free. Many writing festivals are programmed across a weekend, and an all-weekend pass can be expensive; we wanted to make sure that our festival was accessible to people with childcare or employment constraints who might not be able to give up a whole weekend for a series of events.

Our vision for the festival was of a diverse and broad interpretation of creative writing across many forms. As well more traditional events about poetry or novel writing, we programmed sessions on screenwriting for TV, writing comedy, songwriting, writing audio drama, and exploring how new digital and social media can be used to communicate story to new audiences.

Most of the events were fully booked, and none were less than two-thirds full. Although we recognised that it was our first year and that it is important to grow audiences, and that our approach of one off events rather than a fully-programmed

SUNDERLAND
LITERATURE +
CREATIVE WRITING
FESTIVAL 2016

"There is a feeling of being part of an important change. A response to a need to share and act creatively"

couple of days might affect willingness to travel, one of our aims was to draw in visitors from outside the city and to start to establish the Festival as a regional presence. We were therefore delighted to see from our feedback that we had bookings not just from the Wearside area, but also from County Durham, Newcastle and Gateshead, and North Tyneside, and in one case from over fifty miles from Sunderland. The feedback from our visitors has been excellent, and shown a real enthusiasm for the value of our programme and for the desirability of future events.

We deliberately set out to create a programme that blended nationally recognised names with local talent. We staged large events with industry and artistic experts such as a panel discussion on crime writing with best-selling novelists Ann Cleeves and David Mark, on approaches to publication with senior editor Catherine Richards (Pan Macmillan) and agent Julia Churchill (AM Heath), and on poetry with one of Britain's leading poets, Sean O'Brien. We also ran small workshops using local talent to work closely with aspiring writers on idea development, on writing audio drama and very short fiction, on self-publishing and on creative use of social media to tell story. These smaller workshops brought hands-on writing development for those attending, but also contributed to skills development and career enhancement for those designing and delivering the workshops.

Linking concept to practice is a critical part of writing development, and we staged two events in which we worked to make this happen. Our 'Comedy Writing' night brought in four leading comedians with track records in TV sitcom, stand-up and stage. The first half of the event was a panel discussion in which the comedians talked about their approaches to the craft of writing comedy, and took questions from the audience. We then opened up the event to the general public, and each comedian performed a stand-up set, so those who had been at the workshop could see how the theory translated into practice. We took a similar approach to a workshop on songwriting for young people, in which locally-based but nationally and internationally recognised

artists worked with young people on crafting songs, and then played a set afterwards.

Our audiences for a festival in its first year exceeded our expectations, and the feedback from those attending events has been overwhelmingly positive. We were thrilled with the diversity of our audience, from location to age (one event seeing participants under 20 and over 80) to ethnicity, and would hope to grow this in any future events. Part of the mission for the festival was to strengthen the feeling that there is a community of writers in the city, to bring new people into that community (we now have people attending our writers' groups who were not before, thanks to the exposure of the Festival), and to try to foster greater peer networking and support for writers in the city beyond the Festival and into the future. While pleased with its successes, we believe that this gives us a platform to stage future events that are even more ambitious and far-reaching in impact.

There is still much more to do. The groups described in this chapter are working – individually and collectively - to further establish a lasting, inclusive grassroots culture of creative writing in the city, that will inspire and support both those already writing and those who would like to try writing and to discover their potential. That culture will develop a supportive community of writers, which will bring opportunities for collaboration, networking and support.

"There is a feeling of being part of an important change. A response to a need to share and act creatively." (Hester)

Most of all, we are working so that those who are part of that community feel a sense of ownership – that this writing culture belongs to those who are part of it, who will shape and lead its direction into the future, and ensure that Sunderland's culture of creative writing transcends and outlasts the contribution of any one individual or group. In parallel with other cultural activity across the city, it will continue to evolve, develop and grow, and support the writers and aspiring writers of Sunderland, not in isolation but in a way that is deeply integrated with other cultural activity across the city.

Wonderlands

Wonderlands, the UK Graphic Novel Expo, had its inaugural year in 2015 with an event that saw graphic novelists, writers and artists from around the globe come to Sunderland to discuss their art and their industry. Curated by renowned graphic novelist Bryan Talbot, Wonderlands focuses on the graphic novel as an art form, offering an opportunity for independent graphic novelists whilst still catering to fans of well-known titles from the likes of Marvel and DC.

Featuring a series of workshops, a publishers' hall and a programme of presentations covering all aspects

of the industry, Wonderlands is presented in collaboration between the Sunderland Music, Arts and Culture Trust and the University of Sunderland.

In previous years, Wonderlands has featured contributions from artists including Posy Simmonds, Steve Bell, Dave Gibbons, Jeff Anderson, Yomi Ayeni, Doug Braithwaite, David Hine and Metaphrog. A free event, Wonderlands also features a programme of work in schools and at Sunderland College that has seen young people in the city given the opportunity to interact with and learn from award winning artists.

SUNDERLAND
CITY OF CULTURE
BID 2021

THE GRAPHIC NOVEL MAN
THE COMICS OF BRYAN TALBOT

WONDERLANDS
THE U.K. GRAPHIC NOVEL EXPO

SATURDAY MAY 28TH 2016
10AM- 6PM

FREE ENTRY

MAIN GUESTS:
STEVE BELL • **DOUG BRAITHWAITE**
BRYAN TALBOT • **KARRIE FRANSMAN**
DAVID HINE

SPEAKERS AND AUTHORS:
PAUL GRAVETT, MEL GIBSON, SUY VARTY, TOMI AYENI, MARY
TALBOT, SHA NAZIR, LAURENCE GROVE, WOODROW PHOENIX,
METAPHROG, TIM PILCHER, TIM PERKINS, KATE CHARLESWORTH,
JORDAN SMITH, UNA, DARRYL CUNNINGHAM, CONNOR BOYLE,
LIZZIE BOYLE, IAN CULBARD, PAUL REGISTER, KEN MCFARLANE,
WENDY WOOD, NICKOLAS BROKENSHIRE, MARK STAFFORD

PUBLISHERS AND OTHER GUESTS:
ANALOGUE PRESS, MYRIAD EDITIONS, DISCONNECTED PRESS,
2000AD, PAPER JAM COLLECTIVE, SUNDERLAND WATERSTONES,
SUNDERLAND LIBRARY SERVICES, SUNDERLAND UNIVERSITY,
DAMNED FINE ART

FILM SCREENING OF **FUTURESHOCK:
THE STORY OF 2000AD**

METAPHROG'S **'CREATE YOUR OWN
COMIC'** WORKSHOP FOR AGES 11+

FULL PROGRAMME OF TALKS, DISCUSSIONS AND WORKSHOPS
AVAILABLE AT **WWW.WONDERLANDS.ORG.UK**
FOLLOW US ON TWITTER @GNWONDERLANDS

**UNIVERSITY OF SUNDERLAND, CITYSPACE, CITY CAMPUS,
CHESTER ROAD, SUNDERLAND SR1 3SD**
NEAREST MAINLINE STATION: SUNDERLAND NEAREST METRO: UNIVERSITY

A Walk In The People's Park.

WORDS BY *KEITH GREGSON*

A Walk In The People's Park

"Awarded the Briggs and Stratton Britain's Best Park title"

They've a town that's often praised
And both Pier and Park they've raised
And examples set to others far and near
Lines from 'Lads on the Wear' - a
Wearside song from the 1860s

In 2008 Mowbray Park or Gardens, (the 'Peoples' Park of Sunderland), was awarded the Briggs and Stratton Britain's Best Park title. It was a fitting award for one of the country's oldest public parks and a facility whose merit was judged on 'environment, design, usability, access, maintenance and community involvement'. Mowbray Park has been used by the people of Sunderland for over a century and a half and, significantly, much of the praised community involvement has been of a cultural nature. Opened in the 1850s and extended in the following decade, the park was returned to its Victorian splendour around the Millennium. Part of the

millennium development involved a considerable flagging up of the cultural importance of monuments and sculptures ancient and modern and a walk around the park today confirms this.

The main entrance to the park lies close to the heart of the city centre to the north west of the park itself and just behind the entrance to the city's award-winning Museum and Winter Gardens. The park's artistic wrought iron gates were designed around the millennium by Sunderland born Wendy Ramshaw. Wendy has a reputation beyond the city for her jewellery and the geometric design of the gates reflects her own feelings about her native place and its industrial past.

Just inside park gates lies the park lake and at the opposite eastern side of this stands an older piece of art of considerable historic significance. It is statue of mother and deceased child and dedicated to the victims of the Victoria Hall disaster of 1883. (The hall, a large concert hall, stood

THE GRAPHIC

AN ILLUSTRATED WEEKLY NEWSPAPER

No. 708.—Vol. XXVII.
Reg.d at General Post Office as a Newspaper

SATURDAY, JUNE 23, 1883

WITH EXTRA SUPPLEMENT

PRICE SIXPENCE
Or by Post Sixpence Halfpenny

1 Exterior View of the Victoria Hall.—2. External Door of the Hall.—3. The Portion of the Staircase Where the Disaster Occurred, Showing the Partly Open Door Which Caused the Accident (The Dotted Line Shows the Height to Which the Children's Bodies Were Heaped Behind the Door and on the Staircase).—4. Another View of the Scene of the Disaster, Showing the Short Flight of Sixteen Steps Leading to the Fatal Door.

THE INTERIOR OF THE VICTORIA HALL

THE TERRIBLE DISASTER AT SUNDERLAND

just across the road from the park and was destroyed be enemy action in the Second World War). Although a local event in many ways, the tragic Victoria Hall disaster was of great importance and had national consequences. One hundred and eighty three children were trampled to death at a show exclusively for youngsters. As free gifts were being thrown into the stalls, those seated up 'in the gods' rushed down the stairs to join in only to be met by a door which would only partly open. Those who died in the scramble were either crushed or suffocated. There were hardly any adults in the building beyond the performers and one or two local staff although tickets for the show had been sold and advertised around schools. After a review of the disaster, (the papers for which can be seen in The National Archives at Kew), changes were made both in regard to the chaperoning of children at public events and the functioning of doors in buildings used extensively by the public. It is now generally recognised that events in Sunderland led to the introduction of the

'emergency exit' style of door which would swing open when pressure was exerted on a bar extending across it. The statue was initially in the park, later removed, then restored after the Millennium under a protective glass case.

A journey round the southern part of the lake brings visitors to a modern sculpture with a possibly mythical literary pedigree. It is a life-size model of a walrus which was sculpted by artist Andrew Burton at the Millennium. There was a stuffed walrus in the museum during the late Victorian period and rumour had it that, due to Lewis Carroll's family connections with Sunderland, this was the origin of his tale of the Walrus and the Carpenter. There is now some doubt about the truth of this tale – (a matter of timing apparently) – but the legend, if legend it is, has entered local culture. The original walrus was brought to the city by intrepid explorer Joseph Wiggins who has a place in national history through his exploration of the Kara Sea.

"This is an important and much visited area of a city which marks remembrance day in a manner matched by few others"

Not far from the walrus statue and standing between the edge of the park and Burdon Road is the city's war memorial constructed and dedicated in 1925 but since then extended by numerous surrounding panels recalling the fallen of the city beyond the two great wars of the twentieth century. This is an important and much visited area of a city which marks Remembrance Day in a manner matched by few others. This is hardly surprising as Sunderland has always supported membership of the forces massively in relation to the size of its population. Its links to the front line Durham Light Infantry during the First World War meant serious losses in the Battles of Ypres and the Somme. The Fall of Singapore in the Second World War led to the surrender of a fledgling Wearside based artillery unit and subsequent imprisonment for many in Japanese Prisoner of War Camps.

This northern part of the park is essentially the early extension and on its south terrace are couple of rose arbours created in the early 21st century by local blacksmith Craig

Knowles. They were built for courting couples and have a poem etched thus inside them:

If love was a lion, it would purr like a lion, burn bright as Orion.
If love was a rose, we'd watch how it grows, learn all the secrets it knows.

Just south of these on a path (and former railway track) marking the boundary between the original park and its extension is a modern construction linking poetry and sculpture. This is based on the tale of a man who came to the land eventually covered by the park and discovered a toad with a lump of diamonds on its head. The moral? Riches can be found in the most surprising circumstances!

On a crafted slate are inscribed the words –

In the silver mirror of the moon will you find a toad throat shining with diamonds?

The path on which the sculpture stands is sunken and an ornate bridge linking the original park and its extension crosses it. Visitors are instantly met by the sight of the craggy lofty sides of the quarry known as 'Bildon' or 'Building Hill'. Before the park was constructed the hill was used as its name suggests as a source of local stone. The hill and a small grassy knoll to the west are dominated by two nineteenth century statues. The one on the top of hill is of locally born Henry Havelock who raised the siege of Lucknow during the so-called Indian Mutiny of the mid Victorian period. He died of disease in India soon after. The statue actually predates the park and visitors may recognise the figure as it is the same one that resides on one of the four plinths that surround Nelson's Column in Trafalgar Square – an honour for Sunderland indeed.

Keith Gregson

A Walk In The People's Park

"The tale of Jack Crawford and his statue relates well to a consistency in Sunderland's cultural and artistic development."

The other statue celebrates the deed of a local hero who gave rise to a famed saying in the English language – namely 'the nailing of one's colours to the mast'. That is exactly what Wearside born sailor Jack Crawford did at the naval Battle of Camperdown in 1797. Serving on board the admiral's flagship and either under orders or voluntarily Jack shinned up the mast to place the flag back after it had been shot down by enemy fire. In naval terms the lowering of a flag represented surrender so it was important that the rest of the fleet should see that this was not the case. After the battle, Crawford was feted with a medal, a pension and, later, an invitation to follow the coffin at Nelson's funeral. Sadly he was the first man in the town (and possibly the country) to die in the cholera outbreak of 1832.

The tale of Jack Crawford and his statue relates well to a consistency in Sunderland's cultural and artistic development. In the late eighteenth and early nineteenth century, the town had a reputation for its ceremonial pottery and there is a lively gallery in the museum north of the park dedicated to this most fascinating and personal of arts. Here there are many examples of ceremonial pots and ceramics featuring Crawford carrying out his deed – and an equal number dedicated to the opening of the first major bridge across the Wear around the same time. Jack's statue in the park was unveiled towards the end of the nineteenth century but today it is possible to sit and view it through an innovative piece of modern art. As a written guide to the park notes:

A new stone sculpture was created in 1999 to enhance the original statue. This reads: 'on open sea or dry land, nail your colours to the mast'. This piece was created by stonemason Alec Peever.

Widening the cultural theme, Jack's life and bravery has also been celebrated in a couple of modern songs – one is a children's song set to the north eastern tune, The Keel Row. It has the simple chorus

Jack he was a Sunderland lad, a Sunderland Lad, a Sunderland lad

Jack he was a Sunderland lad, a Sunderland Lad was he

The other, by prolific songwriter Johnny Handle, is well known around the country's folk clubs and has been recorded on at least one occasion. Fairly recently an event was held in the park celebrating the heroism of Jack. It finished with an enthusiastic crowd of local people belting out the songs at the base of the statue. Jack has given his name to a room used for cultural events in the museum and also to a building used for local government administration.

The park also has a reputation for both its flowers and its bandstand. Both were recognised soon after the opening of the park extension in the 1860s when the author of the song 'The Sunderland Trip' took his girlfriend into the park:

When in the Park among the flowers, She say, 'Man this is grand

And heaven will surely be like this – if they take in the Bobby's band'

And the Bobby's (Police) Band is not the only group of musicians to have performed in the bandstand across the years. In fact the bandstand has been a centre of constant cultural activity as witnessed by events since the Millennium. In 2010 there was a series of folk concerts organised here. The park also saw an outdoor performance of Twelfth Night by the Mad Alice Theatre Company. Their version of the bard's play was set in the 1960s and involved a shipwreck off the north east coast. It was a mobile performance with the audience following the actors from scene to scene around the park. The park has also often proved a popular venue for outdoor performances of Shakespeare's plays.

The reading of other chapters in this book will confirm the importance given to the development of young musicians in the city. For a number of years those involved in encouraging popular music with teenagers have used the park and bandstand for an annual show of talent. This show has been called by various names and has usually involved much-admired youth mentor 'The Mackem Folksinger' Dave Murray. In 2015, the local newspaper wrote about a 'Smile Concert' and listed young bands and solo artists including Fire Lady Luck, Tammy Proctor, Bad Love, Peter Carmody, Trinity, Corine Andrews, North Divide, Illuminate and The Abyss.

Even younger musicians are given the opportunity annually to display their talents in the park – usually with a theme and based around preparation in schools. This has been going on for over a decade. In 2009, for example, the theme was 'The Singing City' and the songs featured came from the book of that name recently launched. In 2014, the theme was Keep the Home Fires Burning with the children performing songs to celebrate the centenary of the outbreak of the First World War. The performance included old favourites such as 'Keep the Home Fires Burning', 'It's Long Way to Tipperary' and 'Pack up Your Troubles'. The local press noted:

The annual outdoor concerts are held to give pupils from different schools the chance to perform live from the bandstand to a large public audience of friends, family and visitors to the park. They are the result of the successful partnership between the city's museums and School Music Education Hub.

The park and bandstand has also been a base for a series of Vintage and Retro Festivals in recent years. Live music from the 40s, 50s and 60s was accompanied by a show of classic vehicles and the provision of appropriate refreshments. All this was linked to further vintage events such as hairdressing and beauty demonstration from the period and a dressing up photo booth inside the nearby museum. In 2104, part of the park was used for the popular music based Split Festival which had previously been held slightly further south at the Ashbrooke Sports Ground. This festival was renowned for mixing local bands with those with a wider reputation.

A Walk In The People's Park

Keith Gregson

"Nailing your colours to the mast"

A Walk In The People's Park

This festival has Sunderland's Hyde and Beast, Tyneside's Maximo Park, the Cribs and UK hip hop super star Dizzee Rascal. During the following year, youngsters were invited to bring their own teddy bears to a Teddy Bears' Picnic hosted by a music and dance theatre company and involving the youngsters themselves in practical arts and crafts.

During the mid-Victorian period, the powers that be had realised that the blossoming town and port of Sunderland needed an outdoor venue where its ordinary citizens could enjoy a spot of culture and recreation. More recently the 21st century 'powers that be' have been equally active in ensuring the continuity of this realisation, always aware that there still remains room for improvement.

Historic Churches of Sunderland

St Peter's Church

St Peter's Church standing on the north bank of the Wear, is the oldest church in Sunderland, and one of the oldest churches in Britain. It was founded in 674AD as the first part of the Monkwearmouth-Jarrow Monastery, with St Paul's at Jarrow being added in 682AD. The founder of the monastery was Sunderland's patron saint, Benedict Biscop. It was built on land designated for the purpose by the King of Northumbria, Egfrith. Together, St Peter's and St Paul's formed what was described by Biscop as "one monastery in two places". This monastery went on to be one of the greatest centres of learning in Europe at the time, and its most famous pupil was Bede. Biscop brought craftsmen from across Europe to construct his church, including glaziers who constructed some of the first stained glass windows in Britain, and giving Sunderland the honour of being the birthplace of British stained glass. Some of the original stained glass is still there. The church which stands on the site today retains many Anglo-Saxon features, including the tower and the west wall of the church. It has been through several refurbishments and renovations since Biscop's time, but it still retains the unique character which it possessed over thirteen hundred years ago. It is a monument to the vast importance of Sunderland to Europe's medieval history, and it is fitting that the campus of the University which stands close to it has taken its name.

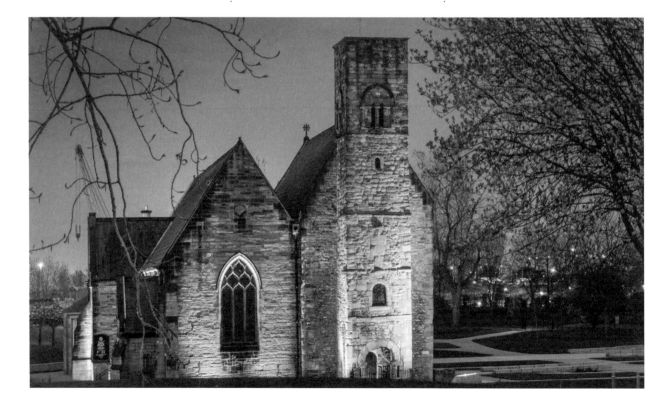

Holy Trinity

Holy Trinity was Sunderland's parish church and is one of the oldest and most interesting buildings in the East End of the City. The church was consecrated on September 5 1719 and the first rector, Daniel Newcombe appointed. There are very few churches from this period in history - the Georgian period. Holy Trinity was designed by the architect William Etty of York. It is constructed of small dark hand-made bricks. Inside, there are tall Corinthian columns, broken pediment and cherubic heads that are extravagantly ornate and unusual. For many years, the church played an important role in the parish - not only was it a place of worship but it became the heart of local government. By 1988, the church was in need of urgent, structural repairs which would be very costly to undertake. So, the decision to hand the church over to the Redundant Churches Fund was made and the last service was conducted on June 26th 1988. The Churches Conservation Trust recently took over Holy Trinity and will save this nationally important building in time for its 300th anniversary in 2019. It will be used as 'The Canny Space', a new community and commercial venue and exciting heritage attraction – one that will interpret and retell 300 years of history and stories through fun, immersive experiences. This ambitious project will re-establish the church as a central part of Sunderland peoples' lives and it will be a key project in the city's heritage led regeneration.

Richard Callaghan

St Andrew's Church, Roker

Described as the "Cathedral of the Arts and Crafts Movement", St Andrew's Church in Roker was completed in 1907. Architect and leading theorist Edward Schroeder Prior regarded St Andrew's as his masterpiece, whilst the interior of the church boasts pieces from great proponents of the Arts and Crafts Movement. These include a tapestry of Edward Burne-Jones' design, produced by Morris & Co, with ornaments, pulpit and altar rails provided by Ernest Gimson and the two main windows designed by Henry Payne. Funded by local shipbuilder John Priestman in memory of his mother, St Andrew's was intended to hold seven hundred people, with instructions to ensure that each had an uninterrupted view of the pulpit and good acoustics throughout. The result is one of the most imposing churches in the region, simultaneously a building of international significance and local importance. A building intended to be at the heart of the growing community in Roker, the simplicity of the church's facade combined with the remarkable beauty of its interior decoration present a startling and remarkable contrast on the northern fringe of the city. A Grade I listed building, and one of Sunderland's hidden gems, St Andrew's Church remains one of three parish churches in Monkwearmouth, alongside St Peter's and All Saints churches.

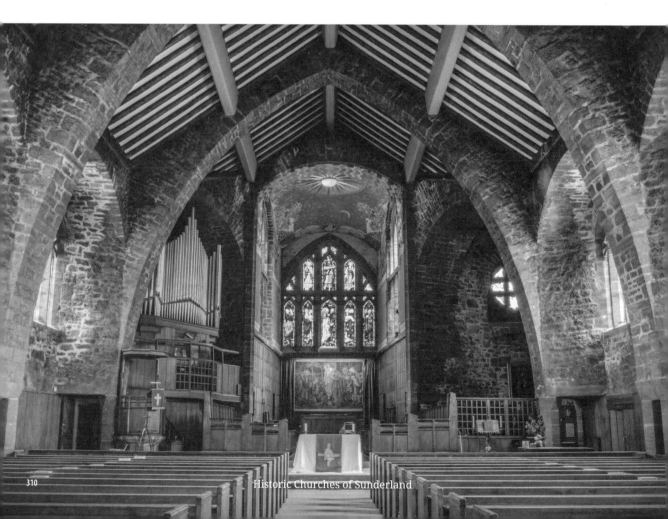

Sunderland Minster

The site of Sunderland Minster, a Grade II* listed building,, in Bishopwearmouth, has been home to a church for more than a thousand years. Previously known as St Michael's Church, it was renamed the Minster Church of St Michael and All Saints on January 11, 1998, becoming the Minster Church for the City of Sunderland. Benedict Biscop's adoption as Sunderland's patron saint in 2007 saw the addition of his name to the church's title, giving the building its now full name of the Minster Church of St Michael and All Saints and St Benedict Biscop. Although there is no record of a rector for Bishopwearmouth until the thirteenth century, excavations during the 1930s discovered Saxon gravestones, believed to date from the ninth or tenth century, suggesting that there had been a church on the site for some hundreds of years prior to the appointment of the first rector. The current medieval church building was restored and reconstructed over the course of the nineteenth and early twentieth centuries, with the existing church the product of comprehensive work undertaken during the 1930s. It no longer acts as parish church for Bishopwearmouth but instead as a church for the entire City of Sunderland.

"For children and young people, culture can raise aspirations, inspire them to succeed, broaden their horizons and help them understand their own values."

Postscript

Postscript

For me, not just as Leader of the City Council but as a resident of Sunderland, arts and culture play an important role; it improves health and well-being, supports stronger communities and delivers improved outcomes for people and communities.

For children and young people, culture can raise aspirations, inspire them to succeed, broaden their horizons and help them understand their own values. Families grasp the opportunity to have quality time together, doing something that's fun but 'nourishing'. Culture brings generations together, encourages people to get out of the house and experience the rich offer the city has - whether that's theatre, museums, exhibitions, workshops, activities, events, heritage or natural heritage. For those who are marginalised - for whatever reason - culture welcomes all people, all backgrounds, gives them a voice and a way to connect to other people in the city, bringing them into communities and forging new communities of interest. For businesses - and everyone - it helps create prosperity, gives a place a clear sense of identity, clear sense of identity, vibrancy, drives footfall, raises awareness and places Sunderland firmly on the map.

Sunderland is a city with great history and culture and through innovation and creativity we have reinvented ourselves over recent years. Visitors, partners and our communities in particular, recognise that culture must be at the very centre of our society.

In celebrating Sunderland, we are raising awareness and understanding of the diverse cultural offer in the city and opening this up to the widest of audiences.

From parks, open spaces, museums, art galleries, theatres and libraries to a plethora of historical heritage assets and our beautiful coastline, we are rich in culture with so much to offer.

We must work hard to create opportunities that inspire and excite audiences whilst spend time to understand, nourish and grow new ones.

As a city we must never stand still. Our focus is to encourage existing and emerging new artists to carve out their creative career paths so they can thrive and flourish in the cultural sector. We will continue to open up opportunities to establish creative industries in the city, making it easier for new businesses to grow and succeed. It is vital that we continue to support our heritage partners and recognise the knowledge, skills and experience which exists from many of the city's volunteers and from within heritage organisations.

Cllr Paul Watson
Leader of Sunderland City Council

Contributors

David Allan
After many years working as a press photographer and photo-journalist, David continues taking photographs, both in a freelance capacity and for pleasure. He is never happier than when he is out and about with his camera in hand!

Rebecca Ball
Director of Sunderland 2021, Rebecca has led the city's bid for UK City of Culture since January 2016. Formerly she was Director of The Cultural Spring, Sunderland and South Tyneside's Creative People and Places programme which commissioned, developed and produced a number of award winning arts participation and engagement projects.

Paul Callaghan
As Chair of Sunderland's Music, Arts and Culture Trust Paul is committed to the cultural regeneration of Sunderland. He is also a board member of Sunderland Culture Ltd and Chair of Live Theatre.

Richard Callaghan
Part of the Sunderland City of Culture and MAC Trust teams, Richard has been working both on the Sunderland City of Culture bid and the development of the Fire Station and the Music, Arts and Culture Quarter. His writing credits also include: MySunderland, MyScotland, MyLondon, and Harry Watts: The Forgotten Hero, amongst others.

Kam Chera
Founder of the award winning 'Stars on Earth' social enterprise delivering hospitality training for young people with special needs, Kam is an active member of the North East business community, holding a number of board memberships in both professional and community organisations and has delivered key cultural events including Sunderland Diwali, Sunderland Vaisakhi Festivals and Sunderland Mela.

Helen Connify
For twenty years Helen has worked in producer and partnership roles within the cultural and media sectors at BBC, BSkyB, Seven Stories: The National Centre for Children's Books and AN: The Artists Information Company. She is Capacity Building Manager for Sunderland Culture and Coordinator of Sunderland Cultural Partnership.

Peter Darrant
A producer and presenter for the Made Television Network, Peter can be seen nightly presenting Made Television's flagship entertainment show, Lowdown Live, and heard daily hosting the breakfast show on Pride World Radio.

Kristian Foreman
Currently the Marketing & Communications Manager for Sunderland's bid to be UK City of Culture 2021, Kristian also produces cultural events and festivals in Sunderland as part of the Music, Arts, and Culture Trust and is Programming Director of Sunderland Shorts Film Festival.

Helen Green
Having worked in the arts for over 25 years in a variety of roles for producing companies and venues in London, Edinburgh and the North East, Helen took on the role of Director for The Fire Station, Sunderland's newest venue, in 2016.

Keith Gregson
A writer, historian and musician who has published a number of history-related books, both popular and academic, Keith also looks after the archives at Sunderland's Ashbrooke Sports Club and writes regularly for national historical magazines.

Daniel Krzyszczak
As manager of the International Community Organisation of Sunderland, Daniel coordinates and organises many community and culture events and festivals including Made in Poland, Looking East, the Play Poland Film Festival and the Meet Your Neighbour Festival.

Rob Lawson
Born and bred in Sunderland, Rob is a former editor of the Sunderland Echo and editorial director of Northeast Press. He is Chair of Governors at Sunderland College, Chair of the Fourteen charity and is also a Trustee at Grace House.

Carol McKay
is a photography historian, writer and curator. Carol is Programme Manager of NEPN (North East Photography Network) and Senior Lecturer in Photographic History and Theory at the Northern Centre of Photography.

Hannah Matterson
Currently the Events and Development Coordinator for Sunderland 2021, Hannah has worked as an arts fundraiser and event producer for Music, Arts and Culture Trust, The Bunker and is also the volunteer coordinator for Sunderland Shorts Film Festival.

Keith Merrin

Chief Executive of Sunderland Culture and Director of the National Glass Centre, Keith is an experienced cultural leader having previously led two of the region's largest independent museums, Bede's World and Woodhorn, been creative director for Newcastle Gateshead Initiative and worked at a national level as director of operations for nature conservation charity, The Wildlife Trusts.

Ross Millard

Musician and artist, Ross is a touring musician, and a member of Sunderland-based bands, The Futureheads and Frankie and The Heartstrings. He has worked as Musical Director on several theatre projects and he is currently Artistic Director of Summer Streets - a music & community festival held annually in Sunderland.

John Mowbray

Co Chairman of the North East Culture Partnership and Chairman of the University of Sunderland, John is also a Trustee of the MAC Trust and a Director of Sunderland Culture. He previously worked for Northumbrian Water and was President of the North East of England Chamber of Commerce.

Padma Rao

is an artist, Director, ArtsConnect UK and Project Co-ordinator, Sangini and has over 15 years' experience in the arts, governance and community development. She is committed to diversity, equalities and women's issues. Since leaving the Arts Council of England, Padma has set up an art studio/gallery Makaan in South Shields and is part of Creative Women's Collective. A published poet, Padma serves as an advisor on the board of Sunderland 2021.

Amanda Ritson

Is Programme Manager of NEPN (North East Photography Network), commissioning photography and developing opportunities for professional photographic artists. Amanda has worked within the regional cultural sector for over 15 years with previous roles at Arts Council England, International Photography Research Network and Creative Partnerships.

Alistair Robinson

Director of Northern Gallery for Contemporary Art since 2002, following curatorial positions at the Victoria & Albert Museum and National Museum of Photography, and being a trustee of Kettle's Yard, Cambridge Alistair is the co-author of 'Museum Studies', an overview of twenty-first century art museum and gallery politics and practice, published by Routledge.

Iain Rowan

A writer, author of the Bath Novel Award and CWA Debut Dagger shortlisted novel 'One of Us', Iain is Creative Director for the Sunderland Festival of Creative Writing, and runs Sunderland writers' group Holmeside Writers.

Julia Stephenson

works as Head of Arts at National Glass Centre. Her responsibilities include delivering the exhibition, learning and residency programmes and working to develop a new collection of Studio Glass.

Graeme Thompson

Graeme Thompson is Pro Vice-Chancellor at the University of Sunderland responsible for external engagement. He is a former producer and executive at BBC and ITV. Graeme chairs Sunderland's 2021 steering group, Sunderland Culture, The Cultural Spring and the Royal Television Society Education Committee. Born in South Shields, he is a trustee of the Customs House.

Paul Watson

As Leader of Sunderland City Council, Councillor Watson chairs the Cabinet and acts as the Council's lead political spokesman. He also chairs a number of other bodies including the national Key Cities Group, the North East Combined Authority, the Association of North East Councils, the UK Delegation to the European Union Committee of the Regions and the Port of Sunderland Board.

Photographic Acknowledgements

Photographs referenced
DA are by David Allan

Why Culture? Why Sunderland?

p6 DA Sunderland Nile Street Art
p8 DA Sunderland Air Show
p9 DA Royal Philharmonic Orchestra - Elvis
p10 DA Bob Stokoe
p11 DA Roker Selfie
p11 DA Warden Law
p12 DA Sunderland Pride
p13 DA Sunderland Pride
p14 DA The Blue House – Raich Carter
p14 DA Fawcett Street in the rain
p16 DA St Bede's Cross
p17 Summer Streets
p19 The Lake Poets
p19 Summer Streets
p19 DA Roker Lighthouse at sunset
p20 DA Royal Philharmonic Orchestra
Sunderland's Performance Venues
p23 DA Sunderland Empire Theatre
p24 Kate Fox
p25 Washington Arts Centre

Sunderland's Cultural Journey

p26 DA Sunderland Street Art
p28 Robert Soden, Lobster Pots & Wear Bridge, 1991
p29 DA Glass
p30 DA National Glass Centre
p31 DA Fire Station Flambeaux
p32 DA Herrington Country Park
p34 DA Keel Line
p34 Inventors project – Mia Braithwaite-Fogg
p34 DA New Wear

Crossing passing under the Wearmouth Bridge
p36 DA Sculpture Roker North Dock
p39 DA Propellers of the City & the Peacock
p39 DA Red House – Sunderland Sculpture Trail
p40 Sunderland Mela, photo Peter Etheringham
p41 DA Hat
p42 DA Hands

ICOS

p45 ICOS at Seaburn New Year's Day Charity dip
p45 ICOS
p45 ICOS Aonach Eagach, Scotland

Sunderland Cultural Partnership

p46 University of Sunderland performance at Customs House, South Shields, 2013
p48 Grayson Perry, The Agony in the Car Park, 2012, part of The Vanity of Small Differences exhibited at Sunderland Museum and Winter Gardens 2013
p49 Sunderland 10x10 Collaborative Hack Event between 10 businesses and 10 artists, April 2016
p50 Asunder Creative Team (Field Music, Warm Digits, Bob Stanley, Esther Johnson, Hugh Brunt and Royal Northern Sinfonia) during rehearsals at Sage Gateshead, June 2016. Photo Mark Savage
p52 Glass blowing at National Glass Centre, 2014
p55 Poet Rowan McCabe performs North East Rising, part of Sunderland Stages, 2014
p56 Dickson-Sarmiento,

Emotional Leak, National Glass Centre, 2013
p56 Summer Streets Festival, The Cultural Spring, 2014

Made With Pride

p59 Made on the Dancefloor

The Role of Sunderland's University in Culture

p60 Foundation Art and Design in NGC
p62 Robert Soden, St Peter's Campus, 1998
p63 Ceramics
p63 Sunfest
p64 Fine Art Studio
p65 National Glass Centre
p65 Glass sculptures
p65 David Puttnam Media Centre
p67 David Puttnam Media Centre Cinema
p68 Sunfest
p69 Sunfest
p70 Student burning glass flower
p72 Solo dancer with chair
p73 Northern Centre of Photography
p74 National Glass Centre
p75 Sunfest
p75 Exterior of National Glass Centre
p75 Fine Art

Sunderland's Amazing Outdoor Attractions

p76 DA Sunderland Airshow
p77 DA Roker Park
p78 DA Houghton Feast
p79 DA Tall Ships

Regional Partnerships and the Case for Culture

p80 DA Ushaw College
p82 DA Angel of the North
p83 DA Seaton Delaval Hall
p84 DA Durham Cathedral
p84 DA Durham Cathedral Sanctuary Knocker

p86 DA Elba Park miners sculpture
p89 DA Sage Gateshead
p90 DA Willow Miner Burnhall, Durham,

Sangini

p92 Women's group at the opening of the My Diwali Home exhibition photo by Tony Griffiths
p93 Sangini at Roker Light House photo by Tony Griffiths

What makes Sunderland a 'City of Culture'

p94 Great Night Out
p96 Inventors - Family Scooter
p97 Great Night Out
p98 Great North Passion
p100 Great North Passion Sculpture
p103 Cultural Spring Community Workshops
p104 Great Night Out
p106 RUSH
p108 RUSH
p109 RUSH
p110 Cultural Spring Bring the Happy
p112 Mr Drayton's Human Juke Box
p113 Mr Drayton's Human Juke Box
p113 Mr Drayton's Human Juke Box
p114 Cultural Spring Street Art Heroes
p115 Cultural Spring Street Art Heroes
p115 Cultural Spring Street Art Heroes
p116 Inventors – Dominic Wilcox
p116 Inventors Dominic Wilcox workshop
p117 Inventors Logo
p117 Lady Bird Umbrella Being made
p119 Inventors

Photographic Acknowledgements Cont.

Index